YOUNG STUDENTS
Learning
Library®

VOLUME 2

America —
Artificial Respiration

NEWFIELD
PUBLICATIONS
SHELTON, CONNECTICUT

CREDITS

Page 132 NHPA: 134 Bridgeman Art Library; 135 U.S. Capitol Historical Society; 137 Colonial Williamsburg; 141 British Museum; 145 Library of Congress; 146 Canadian High Commission (top right); Peter Newark (middle left); 147 Imperial War Museum (top right); Hulton (bottom left); 148 Popperfoto (to pright); NASA (bottom left); 151 ZEFA; 152 Dutch Tourist Office; 154 Michael Holford (top right); ZEFA (bottom left); 160 Picturepoint; 161 Bettmann Archive; 162 ZEFA; 163 A.G.E. Fotostock; 165 Mansell Collection; 167 ZEFA; 172 ZEFA; 175 C.E.P.A.; 180 Mary Evans Picture Library; 181 Armando Curcio Editore; 182 National Gallery, London; 183 Armando Curcio Editore; 185 Pat Morris; 186 ZEFA; 190 R.I. Lewis Smith; 191 Audubon Society; 193 Pat Morris; 195 ZEFA; 196 Popperfoto (top left); Science Photo Library (bottom right); 197 Panos; 198 Armando Curcio Editore; 199 Armando Curcio Editore; 201 NHPA; 202 Pat Morris; 203 Visual Arts Library; 204 Virginia Division of Tourism; 209 Bruce Coleman (top left); Armando Curcio Editore (bottom right); 211 Sonia Halliday (top); ZEFA (bottom) 212 ZEFA; 213; 215

Hutchison Library; 216 Cambridge University; 217 National Museum, Denmark (top); Armando Curcio Editore (bottom); 218 Allsport; 219 Armando Curcio Editore; 221 Dr. R. Muir; 222 Armando Curcio Editore; 223 Carson Pirie Scott & Company (top left); Armando Curcio Editore (bottom left); ZEFA (bottom right); 224 ZEFA; 226 Bruce Coleman; 227 Armando Curcio Editore; 228 Hutchison Library; 229 National Gallery of Scotland; 230 Michael Holford; 232 ZEFA; 234 ZEFA (top); Phoenix & Valley of the Sun Convention & Visitors Bureau (bottom); 235 Arkansas Dept. of Parks & Tourism; 237 Hot Springs Chamber of Commerce; 239 Seattle Art Museum; 242 NASA; 244 Armando Curcio Editore (top); ZEFA (bottom); 245 Imperial War Museum; 246 ZEFA (top); National Gallery of Art, Washington (bottom); 247 National Gallery of Art, Washington (top); The American Museum in Britain, Bath (bottom); 248 Institute of Arts, Detroit; 249 Michael Holford; 250 Armando Curcio Editore; 252 St. Bartòlomew's Hospital; 254 Bridgeman Art Library; 255 Science Photo Library.

CONTENTS

▲ **AMPHIBIANS,** such as the frog, are creatures that are at home both on dry land and in the water.

This map of America shows the location of three major civilizations before the arrival of Europeans.

NORTH AMERICA

Great Lakes

CENTRAL AMERICA

SOUTH AMERICA

▼ A ceremonial headdress made of parrot feathers and gold ornaments, which would have been worn by an Aztec priest or ruler.

▲ The Chippewas originally lived near the Great Lakes. They made their homes out of branch frames covered with animal hides.

AMERICA

The United States is often called "America," but this name really belongs to the two huge continents of the Western Hemisphere—North America and South America. Part of North America, the seven countries from Guatemala to Panama, is called Central America.

The two continents stretch 9,500 miles (15,288 km) from north to south. Together the continents cover about 28 percent of the Earth's land surface. They vary in width from just 30 miles (48 km) in Panama to more than 4,000 miles (6,440 km) across Alaska and Canada.

Many scientists believe that millions of years ago the land masses of America were joined to the western edge of Europe. Some rock forms of the Appalachian Mountains in North America are similar to the rock forms of the Caledonian Mountains in Scotland. Scientists also believe that the two continents were once separate. Then volcanoes spilled lava that

▲ Relay runners carried official messages throughout the Inca empire of Peru.

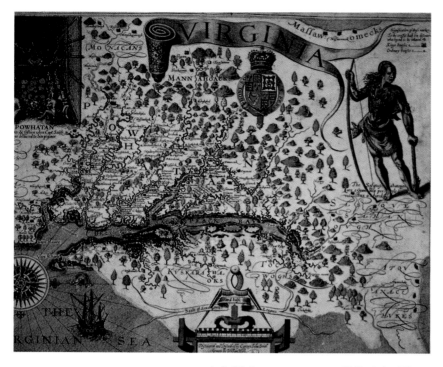

Caribbean islands but thought he was in Asia. A later explorer, Magellan, sailed around the southern tip of the Americas and across the Pacific. Europeans then realized that these lands were two new continents.

An Italian merchant named Amerigo Vespucci persuaded Spanish and Portuguese sea captains to take him along when they visited South America. He returned to Europe and wrote colorful letters claiming he had discovered a new world. One of these letters reached a German geography professor who named the Brazil area *America* (from Amerigo), in honor of Vespucci. The name became popular, and later became the name of both continents.

▶ ▶ ▶ ▶ **FIND OUT MORE** ◀ ◀ ◀ ◀

Central America; Exploration; Native Americans; North America; South America; Vikings

WHERE TO DISCOVER MORE

Krensky, Stephen. *Who Really Discovered America?* Mamaroneck, New York: Hastings House, 1987.

▲ **A 17th century map of Virginia. The first permanent European settlement was founded at Jamestown in 1607, more than 100 years after Columbus first reached the Americas.**

built up the narrow, connecting link known as Central America.

The Americas were explored thousands of years ago by groups of Asian people. Some of them were the ancestors of the Native Americans and Eskimos (Inuits) of today. For centuries, Europeans did not know that the Americas existed. Vikings visited eastern Canada about A.D. 1000, but their settlements died out. In 1492, Columbus reached the

Potatoes, tobacco, corn, tomatoes, lobsters, and other foods were brought back to Europe from America. In return, Europeans introduced pigs, cattle, horses, poultry, and cereal grains. These exchanges greatly shaped the habits of both the Old and the New Worlds.

▶ **Some of the foods 16th century Spanish explorers took back to Europe from the Americas included sunflowers, pineapples, tomatoes, peppers, potatoes, and chocolate. Europeans introduced sugar cane to the West Indies and Brazil, where it quickly became an important cash crop.**

AMERICAN COLONIES

The discovery and exploration of North America caused great excitement among the seafaring people of Europe. They looked upon America as a New World, as a "land of opportunity." Most of all, they saw it as a source of marvelous treasures. Many

of the leading European nations were eager to get the valuable furs, important minerals, and other useful natural resources of North America, so they could grow rich and powerful. They dreamed especially of discovering huge fortunes in gold, silver, and precious gems.

The Spanish were the first in the rush to claim some of the riches of North America. They established the first permanent North American fort at St. Augustine, Florida, in 1565. English colonies were not started until after 1600. The French made a claim to Canada and most of the Mississippi Valley. The Dutch took possession of the lands along the Hudson River, and the Swedes took over the region of land along the Delaware River.

Britain was the most successful of all the nations competing for North America's vast wealth. The colonists from France and Spain were interested mainly in trading with the Native American peoples and taking gold and furs back to Europe. But the

British colonists were determined to set up permanent homes in the New World. In time, Britain gained control of a large area of land along the Atlantic coast including the regions that had first been claimed by the Dutch and Swedes. Britain had established 13 permanent colonies in North America by 1733. In the North were the *New England colonies*—New Hampshire, Massachusetts, Connecticut, and Rhode Island. The *middle colonies* were New York, New Jersey, Pennsylvania, and Delaware. The *southern colonies* were Virginia, Maryland, North Carolina, South Carolina, and Georgia. These colonies declared their independence from Britain in 1776, and after the Revolutionary War, they became the 13 original states that formed the United States of America.

◄ **In September 1620, 41 pilgrims and 61 other English people set sail on the Mayflower for America. The Pilgrims undertook the journey "for the glory of God and the advancement of the Christian faith and honor of our King and country."**

▼ **This map shows the original 13 English colonies.**

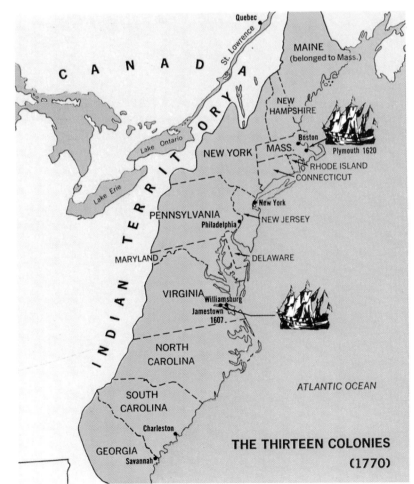

THE THIRTEEN COLONIES (1770)

▲ In the 1600s, the Iroquois of North America united to protect themselves against the threat of invasion by white settlers.

The Early Settlements

A large group of men and boys landed in Virginia in the spring of 1607. They founded the Jamestown Colony, the first permanent British settlement in the New World. A second group of people, the Pilgrims, sailed on the *Mayflower* from Plymouth, England, to the coast of Massachusetts in 1620. There they set up the Plymouth Colony. Puritans came from Britain ten years later to found the Massachusetts Bay Colony, with settlements in Boston and Salem.

Many hardships and dangers awaited these Europeans who first made the long ocean voyage to the New World. North America of the 1600s was a vast wilderness. The colonists had to get used to this strange New World. They had to give up many of their Old World habits of living. Even the kinds of food they were used to eating were no longer available to them.

The Native Americans often lent a helping hand to the colonists. Native Americans had already explored most of the land, and they knew the best ways to travel the waters and cross the mountains. They showed the colonists where to find minerals and other important resources. They also knew all about the kinds of foods that could be found. The Massachusetts colonists had never even heard of corn, squash, and sweet potatoes. The Native Americans showed the colonists how to plant and grow these crops, and to prepare foods such as cornmeal mush, corn pone, hominy, succotash, and popcorn.

But many Native American tribes were not so friendly to the newcomers. They were angry because the new settlers were forcing them out of their homes and hunting grounds. They fought back with all their might. Colonists in Virginia and Massachusetts had to learn to defend their homes and families from attacks.

Not all the early settlers were prepared for the tough and dangerous life in Colonial America. The Jamestown colonists suffered from the burning heat of summer and the damp cold of winter. Some died of starvation and disease. But luckily, most of the early colonists were brave and hardy folk. They were ready to face all hardships in the struggle to build a new life in the land of opportunity. Many Europeans hoped to make new lives in the New World, so the settlement of America grew quickly after the found-

▲ The colonists faced many difficulties in their new country. Everyone shared in the work of establishing a new colony.

ing of the earliest colonies. By 1700, towns were scattered along the whole eastern coast.

The People of the Colonies

Most colonial settlers were English, but others were French, Irish, Scottish, Dutch, German, and Swedish. They all had one thing in common—they wanted to make new lives for themselves. Some were drawn to the New World by the promise of work, because in their home countries they were not able to make a good living. Others were excited by the chance to get some land to call their own. The New World offered land that was cheap or even free. Still others fled Europe because they were not allowed to worship as they wished. They hoped to find freedom of religion in the New World colonies. The Pilgrims and the Puritans had been the first religious groups to come to America for this reason. Others were the Quakers, Roman Catholics, and French Protestants known as Huguenots.

Some Europeans who wanted to settle in the New World were poor

people who did not have enough money to make the trip. So they offered themselves as *indentured servants* to wealthy colonists. An indentured servant agreed to work for his master for a certain number of years. In return, the master agreed to pay for the servant's trip and to provide him with room and board for the period of his service. But not all indentured servants came to America by choice. Some were criminals who had been forced to leave their countries. A few were black people brought from Africa by Europeans. Many more black people were captured in Africa and sold into slavery. Most of the slaves were brought to the southern colonies to work on the farms. Other slaves were taken to the North and put to work in the homes or shops.

Everyday Life

Each one of the three regions—New England, the middle colonies, and the southern colonies—had special conditions that made it different from the other regions. So people in each region developed different ways of living and working.

All the colonies depended on farming. The South was best suited for large-scale farming. The soil was rich and the climate was warm. Many southern colonists lived on

▲ **Bacon's Castle, Virginia, was built in 1655. The Virginia Company was given a charter by King James I in 1606, and English colonists settled in Virginia a year later.**

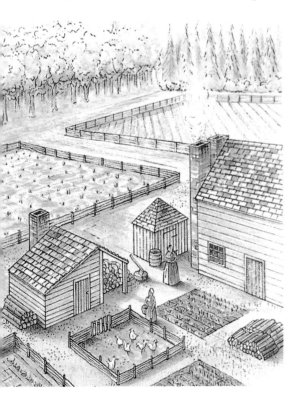

◀ **A small family farm in Maryland in the late 17th century. Farms by now were not just self-sufficient but produced a surplus of tobacco, wheat, and indigo, which were exported to Europe.**

COLONY	FOUNDED	FOUNDER	REASON FOR SETTLEMENT	STATEHOOD
Virginia	1607	Capt. John Smith	Profit and trade	June 25, 1788
Massachusetts	1620	William Bradford	Freedom to be Puritans	Feb. 6, 1788
New York	1626	Peter Minuit	Profit and trade	July 26, 1788
New Hampshire	1630	John Mason	Left Massachusetts because rules were too strict	June 21, 1788
Maryland	1634	George Calvert	Freedom to be Roman Catholics	April 28, 1788
Connecticut	1636	Thomas Hooker	Left Massachusetts because rules were too strict	Jan. 9, 1788
Rhode Island	1636	Roger Williams	Thrown out of Massachusetts because he did not conform to Puritan thinking	May 29, 1790
Delaware	1638	Peter Minuit	Profit and trade	Dec. 7, 1787
North Carolina	1653	Eight Lords Proprietors	Profit and trade	Nov. 21, 1789
New Jersey	1664	John Berkeley and George Carteret	Profit and trade	Dec. 18, 1787
South Carolina	1670	Eight Lords Proprietors	Profit and trade	May 23, 1788
Pennsylvania	1682	William Penn	Freedom to be Quakers	Dec.12, 1787
Georgia	1733	James Oglethorpe	Colonization	Jan. 2, 1788

► Native Americans used wampum, made from shells, to keep records and decorate clothes. It was also used by the colonists as money, especially in the fur trade.

In 1606, the east coast of North America was an almost unbroken wilderness. There were no Europeans except for a small group of Spaniards at St. Augustine, Florida. By 1750, less than 150 years later, there were over 1.5 million men, women and children living in the 13 colonies.

huge plantations where tobacco and rice were grown for export to Britain. Every southern plantation was a tiny village.

The plantation owner, or planter, was mayor, judge, sheriff, preacher, doctor, lawyer, and storekeeper for the community. He and his family often lived in a great mansion. His black slaves lived in small shacks away from the main house. Most of them spent their days at hard labor in the fields. Some were put to work as servants in the planter's home.

Each plantation had its own carpenter, cooper (barrel maker), blacksmith, cobbler (shoemaker), tanner, and other craftsmen who provided the basic needs of everyday life. From the plentiful plantation trees came the wood for the carpenter and the cooper. The blacksmith burned wood for charcoal, the hot coals needed to make horseshoes and other ironware.

Cotton and flax were grown and made into thread for weaving cloth. Cattle supplied milk and meat, as well as skins for the tanner and leather for the cobbler. Sheep's wool was woven or knitted to make clothing and bedding. Some planters were

so rich they did not have to wear homemade clothing. They ordered fine silk gowns, satin breeches, and other fancy clothes from Britain.

The land in New England was rocky, the soil was poor, and the farms were small. Most towns were built as a square of wooden or stone houses facing a *common,* a piece of land shared by the community, on which livestock grazed. Unlike the plantation family, the New England family did not raise crops for export to Britain. Each family grew only enough food for itself. The New Englander hardly ever bought ready-made British goods. People made all their own tools, clothing, and furniture. The North was blessed with rich forests, so there was plenty of lumber. New England woodworkers made especially fine furniture.

The main profit of the northern colonies came not from the land, but from the sea. Fishing, shipbuilding, shipping, and whaling were all important industries. Trading ships made voyages along the Atlantic coast, bringing goods to the other colonies. They also crossed the Atlantic and traded with Europe, Africa, and the West Indies. Whaling ships sailed out of Nantucket, New Bedford, and other New England ports. The voyages sometimes lasted for two or three years. One lasted eleven years!

The middle colonies were known as the "bread" colonies. Their most important export was wheat. They also kept livestock and produced beef, pork, and lamb. Most of the farms were run by single families. But in the Hudson River Valley were large estates where wealthy landowners lived as comfortably as the planters in the South. The rich merchants of the cities also lived in splendid style.

Transportation

The early colonists traveled by foot over the Indian paths and wilderness trails, or they rode horseback. For many years, there were no roads outside cities. People found it easier to travel by water than by land. Vessels sailed regularly up and down the coast from port to port. Inland, large rivers, such as the Hudson, were heavily traveled.

Overland travel became easier as city streets were paved with cobblestones and wilderness trails were made into dirt roads. In 1732, a stagecoach journeyed between New York and Philadelphia in record time—one week. Wealthy colonists imported splendid coaches from Europe. These coaches must have been a grand sight, painted with shiny gold and red paint, and drawn by four prancing horses.

But colonists who walked in the cities did not always have such a grand time. City streets were often used as garbage dumps. Hogs and other animals ran free in New York's streets, looking for food among the garbage. Rich people were able to buy *sedans* to avoid all this. The sedan was an enclosed chair with two poles attached to each side.

Servants or slaves carried the chair, with its rider, on their shoulders.

School and Church

Colonial children helped their parents with everyday chores. But schooling was also an important part of daily life for many children. The three R's—"Reading, 'Riting, and 'Rithmetic"! were the basic lessons taught by every schoolteacher, whether he or she was teaching in a public school or was hired as a private tutor. America's first public schools were in New England. The schools were free, but only boys could attend. Girls were rarely sent to public schools in colonial times. But both boys and girls could attend a "dame" school, run by a woman who taught in her home. The children learned their three R's seated around the kitchen fire. They made their own pens by carving sharp points from goose quills. They boiled bark to make a syrup that they used as writing ink.

On southern plantations, the planter's children were tutored by a schoolmaster who lived with the family for several months of the year. Some boys—and a few girls—were sent to private schools in Europe. The first free school in the South was the grammar school at the College of William and Mary, in Williamsburg, Virginia.

▲ The first elected representatives of the colony of Virginia met at Jamestown in 1619. Together with the governor and council of the colony they fashioned the laws by which the colony was governed.

Going to church was another important part of colonial life. The church was not only a place of worship—it was also the center of community life. People in the South enjoyed staying around the church after the services were over. Adults gathered in groups to chat, while boys and girls played tag or hopscotch or flew kites. However, the mood in New England churches on Sunday was quite different. The Puritans believed that people should be quiet and serious on the Sabbath. Children were not allowed to shout and play. Every Sunday morning, after the drum roll that announced the beginning of church services, every man, woman, and child had to be in his or her seat at the meetinghouse. Sermons often lasted three hours in the morning and another three hours in the afternoon.

▶ The letters issued in 1621 by King James I of England, giving the Pilgrims the right to own the land where they had settled in Plymouth Colony, New England. But it gave them no powers or right to govern their colony.

Recreation

Life in colonial times offered many pleasures as well as duties. Fox hunting, horse racing, and week-long house parties made life fun in the South. New England parties were happy occasions that often combined work and play. Neighbors gathered together to husk corn, make quilts, and even build houses or barns.

Like today's Americans, the early colonists especially enjoyed their holidays. Thanksgiving was first observed by the early settlers at Plymouth. But the colonists did not celebrate Christmas in the way that it is celebrated today, for the Puritans believed that it was wrong to be joyful about religion. Christmas did not become a real holiday until the middle of the 1800s. An important holiday in colonial times was the king's birthday.

In time, however, the links with the old homeland, Britain, became strained. The American colonists wanted more freedom to govern their own affairs. This desire grew stronger and stronger, until the colonists declared their break with British rule. A total of 169 years had passed between the time of the first permanent colony, at Jamestown in 1607, and the Declaration of Independence from Britain in 1776. After the 13 colonies won their right to be an independent nation, a happy day on the American calendar was Independence Day, the Fourth of July.

▶ ▶ ▶ ▶ **FIND OUT MORE** ◀ ◀ ◀ ◀
Agriculture; American History; Declaration of Independence; Jamestown; Mayflower, Mayflower Compact; Pilgrim Settlers; Puritan; Raleigh, Sir Walter; Revolutionary War; *Also read articles on each state listed in table on page 138*

AMERICAN HISTORY

Britain did not start to colonize the east coast of North America until more than a century after Columbus and other explorers had begun exploring the Western Hemisphere. The first permanent British settlement in the New World was started in 1607 at Jamestown in Virginia. The Virginia Colony was governed by a British governor and the "House of Burgesses." The people elected the *burgesses* (representatives) to this assembly beginning in 1619. The Virginia House of Burgesses was the first representative assembly in America.

A second British settlement was started when the Pilgrims landed at Plymouth, Massachusetts, in 1620. The Pilgrims had left home because they were not allowed to worship God in their own way. They were part of a large group of people called *Puritans,* who wanted to "purify" the Church of England. Another group of Puritans founded the Massachusetts Bay Colony at Boston and Salem in 1630. The British had set up 13 colonies along the Atlantic Coast, from Maine to Georgia, by 1733.

Many Native Americans died from diseases, such as smallpox, brought by the Europeans. At first many of the Native American people were friendly to the new settlers. But fights soon broke out because the Native Americans did not want the colonists to take over their lands.

The Roots of Revolution
Wars fought by Spain, France, and Britain caused fighting in several parts of America during most of the 1700s. In America these were called the French and Indian War. Both the French and the British had Indians fighting for them. France lost the French and Indian War, and by 1763 Great Britain had gained nearly all

French land in America, including Canada. The British needed money to pay their war debts. So Parliament decided to tax the colonies. The angry American colonists felt the taxes were unfair, because they had no representatives in Parliament. But even though they protested, King George III and Parliament would not end the taxes. Colonists who took the side of the king were called *Loyalists* or *Tories.* Other colonists wanted independence from Britain. They were called *Patriots.* Still others—probably the majority—had a "wait and see" attitude.

The Patriots felt that Britain was taking away rights that they deserved as free citizens. They therefore defied the British government. This was particularly true in Massachusetts and in the city of Boston, beginning about 1761. By 1765, resistance had spread to other large cities. It continued to grow for ten years.

▲ **A Native American chief drawing from about 1585. As settlers moved westward and took over the most fertile land, they came into conflict with many tribes.**

◀ **In 1492, Christopher Columbus crossed the Atlantic with three small sailing ships: the *Santa Maria*, the *Pinta*, and the *Niña*. The Atlantic crossing took 30 days to complete.**

▲ **Early Puritan settlers in North America. They went there from England so that they could worship God in the way they wanted.**

▲ **Covered wagons, drawn by oxen or horses, carried pioneers westward. Settlers survived by using their hunting and farming skills.**

▶ **How the United States grew from 1776 to 1898.**

The Fight for Independence

In 1774 the first Continental Congress, representing the 13 original colonies, met and denounced the British laws. One night in April, 1775, the Patriots learned that British troops planned to capture guns and ammunition stored by the colonists in Concord, Massachusetts. Leaders of the Patriots were in danger of arrest, so Paul Revere and other Minutemen rode for miles through the darkness to warn them. The Battles of Lexington and Concord the next day marked the beginning of the Revolutionary War.

The fighting lasted for almost seven years, during which George Washington was the commander in chief of the Continental Army. He kept the soldiers of the ill-equipped colonial army together until they won the war in 1781. In the peace treaty, signed in 1783, Great Britain recognized the independence of the United States of America, and turned over to the new country all British lands east of the Mississippi.

A national flag for the new United States was approved on June 14, 1777, during the Revolution. This first flag, the original Stars and Stripes, had one star for each state and 13 stripes to stand for the first 13 colonies.

The new nation needed laws to guide and protect its people. A first attempt at setting up a system of national law was made in the Articles of Confederation, which became law in 1781. But the system did not work, and a new Constitution of the United States was created in 1787. Adopted in 1789, it is still the basic law of the land today. Under the Constitution, a President is elected by the people every four years. George Washington was elected the first President and took office on April 30, 1789.

The Union Expands

Not all Americans were content to live in the settled areas of the East Coast. Looking for land to farm, pioneers began to move west toward the Ohio River even before the Revolutionary War. The land between the Appalachian Mountains and the Mississippi River was quickly settled and divided into states. By 1800, Vermont, Kentucky, and Tennessee had joined the union.

The size of the country was more than doubled in 1803 by the Louisiana Purchase. The U.S., under

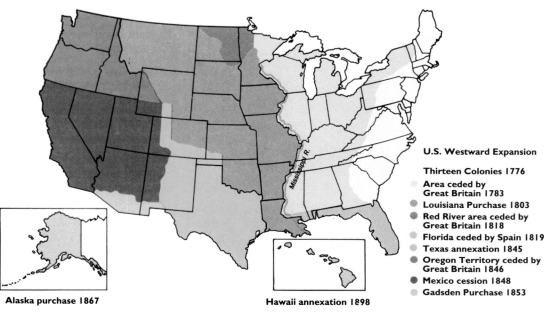

Alaska purchase 1867

Hawaii annexation 1898

U.S. Westward Expansion

Thirteen Colonies 1776
- **Area ceded by Great Britain 1783**
- **Louisiana Purchase 1803**
- **Red River area ceded by Great Britain 1818**
- **Florida ceded by Spain 1819**
- **Texas annexation 1845**
- **Oregon Territory ceded by Great Britain 1846**
- **Mexico cession 1848**
- **Gadsden Purchase 1853**

◀ **The battle of Bunker Hill was the first major battle of the Revolutionary War. The British won, but nearly half of their troops were killed.**

the leadership of President Thomas Jefferson, paid France $15 million for a huge tract of land that extended from the Mississippi River west to the Rocky Mountains, and from New Orleans all the way to Canada. Two young army officers, Meriwether Lewis and William Clark, explored this new land for the U.S. Government. Lewis and Clark traveled beyond the Rockies to the Pacific Ocean. Their glowing reports of the western frontier made many Americans decide to move west.

The United States and Britain went to war again in 1812, fighting over the freedom of U.S. ships at sea. United States troops burned government buildings at York (now called Toronto) in Canada. In August, 1814, the British burned the U.S. Capitol, some other buildings, and the President's House in return for the burning of the buildings in York. President James Madison had the house painted white to cover the scars and smoke stains. The home of the President of the United States has been called the "White House" since that time.

The U.S. continued to grow in size and political power after the War of 1812. Spain sold Florida to the U.S. in 1819. Settlements were founded beyond the Mississippi by pioneers who traveled to the West in wagon trains. Many Americans settled in Texas, which belonged to Mexico at that time. They fought with the Mexicans over laws and boundaries. In San Antonio, in 1836, an entire group of Texan Americans was killed by Mexican soldiers in the Battle of the Alamo. Angry Texans crying, "Remember the Alamo!" defeated the Mexicans a few weeks later. The Texans then went on to win their independence from Mexico. Texas was *annexed,* or added, to the Union as a state in 1845. The U.S. and Mexico fought over this annexation in the Mexican War from 1846 to 1848. The U.S. won. Mexico agreed to sell much of its western land, including California, to the U.S.

QUIZ

1. Who was the last British king to rule part of America?
2. Washington, D.C., became the U.S. capital in 1800. What cities held this honor before then?
3. Place-names all over the U.S. reflect the many different cultures. What does Los Angeles mean?
4. What was the Underground Railroad?
5. What was the last state admitted to the Union?

Answers on page 256

When the original 13 colonies declared their independence in 1776, the United States was only a fourth of its present size. By 1850 it was a nation of 31 states stretching from the Atlantic to the Pacific, and covering an area of 3 million square miles (or nearly 8 million sq. km).

In 1849, gold was discovered in California. Many people, called "Forty-Niners," went west to search for gold. Other travelers to the West went to make new lives for themselves and their families. The trip westward was long and dangerous. The Oregon Trail, which many of these pioneers took, was more than 2,000 miles (3,220 km) long. Attacks by Native Americans troubled almost every wagon train.

The Civil War

In the first half of the 1800s, debate between the North and the South on the question of slavery became more and more bitter. Slaves brought from Africa had been used on the large plantations in the South since colonial times. When cotton became a popular crop, more and more slaves were needed. The South's prosperity was based on the slavery system. In

> When the Civil War began, President Lincoln hoped that he would need only 75,000 volunteers for a few months to put down the uprising. In the end, four million men fought in a cruel war that lasted for four long years.

▲ The battle of Gettysburg, July 1–3, 1863, was a turning point of the Civil War. This important Union victory stopped a Confederate invasion into northern territory.

the North, slavery was not profitable and most Northern states had laws against it. A large group of Northerners believed that slavery was wrong and should not be allowed in new territories. They wanted to *abolish* (get rid of) slavery in the whole country. They were known as *abolitionists*. States' rights became a major issue. The Southern

states saw less and less reason for staying in the Union.

In 1860—the year Abraham Lincoln was elected President—several southern states *seceded* from, or left, the Union and formed a new government. They called themselves the Confederate States of America. They chose Jefferson Davis as their president. The Civil War began on April 12, 1861, when Confederate soldiers fired on Fort Sumter, a U.S. fort in the harbor of Charleston, South Carolina.

Abraham Lincoln remained President of the U.S. throughout the four-year war. General Ulysses S. Grant was the most famous of the commanders of the Union forces. Robert E. Lee was the commanding general of the Confederate army. In this war, brother often fought against brother, and friend against friend. After the North won this long and bloody war, two things were settled—slavery was abolished, and it was clear that no state could leave the Union. Just five days after the Civil War ended, President Lincoln was assassinated in Ford's Theater in Washington, D.C., by John Wilkes Booth, an actor who was a strong supporter of the South.

The Railroad Helps Settle the West

The U.S. went through a period of prosperity for the next 20 years, mostly due to the growth of transportation. Railroads were built, running all the way to the Pacific coast. This opened up the West for further settlement. Cattle raising, land development, lumbering, and silver mining made the western lands prosperous.

But the new settlers, miners, and ranchers posed a serious threat to the Native Americans. The Native Americans were fighting not only for their lives, but for their way of life. They were being driven from their ancient hunting grounds, from the homelands that had been theirs for

generations. One tribe that fought the hardest was the Apache. The Apache War raged in New Mexico, Arizona, and Texas. It lasted almost 40 years, and was probably the bloodiest Indian war. Other serious Indian wars were the Sioux War in North Dakota and South Dakota, Minnesota, and Montana; the Nez Percé War in the Pacific Northwest; and the Modoc War in California.

In the East, where manufacturing had become the most important business, another kind of fight was going on. The long struggle between factory owners and workers had started. Labor unions were seeking better working conditions, higher pay, and shorter hours for workers.

By 1890, there was scarcely any *frontier* (completely unsettled land) left. The nation stretched from the Atlantic to the Pacific. Forty-five states had been formed by the beginning of the 20th century. Three more states came into the Union in the next 12 years. The admission of huge Alaska and distant Hawaii in 1959 brought the number to 50 states.

A World Power
Another war took place before the end of the 1800s. The Spanish-American War, fought with Spain in 1898 over Cuba's independence, began when a U.S. battleship, the *Maine*, was blown up in the harbor of Havana, Cuba. America won this brief conflict, and the world began to realize that the young country was becoming a power to reckon with.

Under President Theodore Roosevelt, the U.S. dug the Panama Canal, which made it possible for ships to go from the Atlantic to the Pacific without going around stormy Cape Horn at the southern tip of South America.

World War I started in Europe in 1914. Germany fought against France and Britain. America did not

◄ **The railroad opened up North America. Railroad posters of the 1800s confidently predicted the linking of the whole continent.**

▼ **Between 1830 and 1910, 28 million immigrants entered America. Most were Europeans who came to escape poverty and unemployment at home.**

A TIMETABLE OF AMERICAN HISTORY

The history of America starts with the history of the Native Americans. A tribe of the Pacific Northwest carved this bird's head.

In the early 1600s, people like the Pilgrims settled in America, hoping to build a better life.

In 1908 Henry Ford and other automakers sent a nation off on a new craze —the automobile.

A 1962 cartoon showing the former U.S.S.R.'s leader Nikita Khrushchev and the U.S. President John F. Kennedy arm-wrestling for power on top of nuclear weapons.

B.C.
18,000 Ancestors of Native Americans arrive from Asia.

A.D.
1000 Vikings land in North America.
1492 Christopher Columbus lands in the New World.
1607 English settlers founded Jamestown.
1620 Pilgrims founded Plymouth (Plimouth) Colony.
1754–1763 The French and Indian War leaves Britain in control of most of eastern North America.
1770 The Boston Massacre.
1773 The Boston Tea Party.
1774 The First Continental Congress meets in Philadelphia.
1775 The American Revolution begins with the battles of Lexington and Concord.
1776 The Declaration of Independence.
1781 American troops defeat British troops at Yorktown, Virginia.
1783 Britain recognizes U.S. independence.
1788 The Constitution comes into effect.
1789 George Washington is elected first President.
1791 The Bill of Rights becomes part of the Constitution.
1803 The Louisiana Purchase.
1812–1815 The War of 1812.
1819 Spain cedes Florida to the U.S.
1823 The Monroe Doctrine warns against European interference in the Americas.
1825 The Erie Canal is completed.
1836 Texas declares independence from Mexico.
1846–1848 The Mexican War. The U.S. gains part of Arizona, New Mexico, Colorado, Nevada, Wyoming, Utah and California.
1861–1865 The Civil War.
1863 Abraham Lincoln issues the Emancipation Proclamation.
1865 President Lincoln is assassinated. The 13th Amendment outlaws slavery.
1867 The U.S. buys Alaska from Russia.

1869 The transcontinental railroad is completed.
1898 The U.S. defeats Spain in the Spanish-American War.
1914 The Panama Canal is opened.
1917 The U.S. enters World War I.
1918 World War I ends; President Woodrow Wilson's Fourteen Points form the basis of peace negotiations.
1920 The 19th Amendment gives women the right to vote.
1929 A stock market crash begins the Great Depression.
1933 President Franklin D. Roosevelt introduces his New Deal program.
1941 After the Japanese attack Pearl Harbor, the U.S. enters World War II.
1945 The U.S. drops two atomic bombs on Japanese cities; World War II ends.
1948 Congress approves the Marshall Plan.

1950–1953 The Korean War.
1954 The Supreme Court rules racial segregation in public schools is illegal.
1962 The U.S.S.R. removes its missiles from Cuba ending the Cuban Missile Crisis.
1963 Martin Luther King Jr. leads a civil rights march on Washington, D.C. President John F. Kennedy is assassinated.
1965 President Lyndon B. Johnson orders U.S. troop buildup in Vietnam.
1969 Neil Armstrong becomes the first person on the moon.
1973 The last American soldiers leave Vietnam.
1974 Richard M. Nixon is the first President to resign from office.
1987 The U.S. and the U.S.S.R. sign the first comprehensive nuclear arms control treaty.
1989 U.S. troops invade Panama and depose military leader Manuel Antonio Noriega.
1991 The Persian Gulf War.
1992 The U.S. sends troops to Somalia to help distribute food to the famine-ridden nation.

want to enter this war at first. But events forced the country to fight. President Woodrow Wilson urged Congress to declare war on Germany in April 1917. With American troops helping out, Germany was defeated by the allies (America, France, and England) in 1918.

For more than ten years the world tried to recover from the debts and social changes brought about by the war. But finally there was a world-wide economic depression. The Depression began in Germany in the early twenties and reached the U.S. in 1929. Many people did not have jobs or money during this time to buy food or clothing. The government started many new building projects to make work so that people could earn at least some money. Highways, dams, bridges, and public buildings were constructed. Social Security and other welfare programs were begun.

The U.S. was at peace with the rest of the world for 20 years after World War I. Then in 1939 World War II broke out in Europe. Germany, under Adolf Hitler and his Nazi party, aided by Italy, attacked and captured many

European and North African countries. The U.S. did not want to enter another world war. But Japan, an ally of Germany, bombed the American naval base at Pearl Harbor, Hawaii, on December 7, 1941. Congress declared war on Japan, Germany, and Italy. The war ended in Europe in May 1945 when the Germans surrendered. Japan did not surrender until August of that year, after the U.S. had dropped the first atom bombs on two Japanese cities.

One of the results of World War II was the organization of the United Nations. Nearly all the countries of the world belong to the UN. The representatives of the member nations work together to try to solve world problems. When war broke out between the North and South Koreans in 1950, the UN sent troops to defend the South Koreans from the North Korean Communists. The U.S. gave the largest share of troops and equipment.

In spite of its war efforts, the United States had become more and more prosperous. Americans enjoyed

▲ **A B17 Flying Fortress of the 15th U.S. Army Air Force releasing its bombs north of Budapest, Hungary during World War II.**

The annual income of 250 million Americans is roughly equal to the total income of all the three billion people of Asia, Africa, and South America.

◄ **During the Depression years of the 1930s, hunger and unemployment brought hardship to many Americans, especially farmers who faced falling prices and drought.**

▶ **U.S. soldier with a Vietnamese child. The Vietnam War was one of the great issues troubling the nation in the 1960s and early 1970s.**

▼ **In 1969, the American astronaut Neil Armstrong became the first person to set foot on the moon.**

a higher standard of living than any other people on Earth. Industry grew steadily throughout the 1950s.

Because of its position as the world's strongest and richest nation, the United States played a leading part in world affairs. Its main rival in foreign affairs was the U.S.S.R. This rivalry became known as the "Cold War." In the 1950s and 1960s U.S. personnel were sent to help the South Vietnamese in their war against the Communist North Vietnamese. By 1965 U.S. troops were fighting in Vietnam. The Vietnam War led to discontent at home. A peace accord was signed in 1973, to conclude the longest and unhappiest overseas war fought by Americans.

On July 20, 1969 two U.S. astronauts became the first men to walk on the moon. The U.S. has continued to advance in space technology, despite setbacks to its manned shuttle program. U.S. achievements in communications, computers, laser science, and microbiology in particular have been considerable.

In the late 1980s the Cold War ended when the communists lost control of the U.S.S.R., which broke up into independent, democratic republics.

In 1991 the U.S. was involved in the Persian Gulf War. U.S. troops helped to free the Mideast nation of Kuwait, which had been invaded by its neighbor, Iraq.

▶▶▶ **FIND OUT MORE** ◀◀◀
Government see Articles of Confederation; Cabinet, U.S.; Constitution; U.S. Flag; United States Government
Life see American Colonies; Black Americans; Exploration; Hispanic Americans; Native Americans; Pioneer Life
Major Events see Civil Rights Movement; Civil War; Depression;

French and Indian War; Gold Rush; Indian Wars; Korean War; Mexican War; Persian Gulf War; Reconstruction; Spanish-American War; Vietnam War; War of 1812; World War I; World War II
Also read articles on each state and each President.

AMERICAN INDIANS

SEE NATIVE AMERICANS

AMERICAN LITERATURE

SEE LITERATURE

AMERICAN REVOLUTION

SEE REVOLUTIONARY WAR

AMINO ACID

SEE PROTEIN

AMOEBA

Every time you drink a glass of water you swallow several amoebas. These creatures are made up of only a single cell—unlike ourselves; each of us contains many millions of cells. Amoebas are found in both saltwater and freshwater and in the soil. They also live inside human beings and animals. Most types are harmless, but one variety can cause a disease called amoebic dysentery in human beings. Amoebas vary in size from about ⅟₁₀₀ inch (0.25 mm) to ⅟₁₀ inch (2.5 mm).

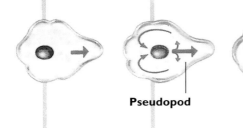

Pseudopod

An amoeba moves from place to place by pushing out part of itself. The pushed-out part is called a *pseudopod*. The amoeba pours the rest of its body fluids into the pseudopod, and so moves itself along. It also uses pseudopods to swallow tiny bits of food.

Amoebas reproduce by splitting. The nucleus of the original amoeba divides into two parts. Then the amoeba itself splits, forming two new amoebas, each with its own nucleus.

▶ ▶ ▶ ▶ **FIND OUT MORE** ◀ ◀ ◀ ◀
Cell

AMPERE, ANDRE-MARIE (1775–1836)

André Ampère was a French mathematician and scientist who studied electricity and magnetism. He was born at Polemieux, near Lyons, France. His father was beheaded during the violence of the French Revolution when André was 18. A few years later, André's wife died of tuberculosis. He was greatly depressed by the loss of his wife and father and tried to forget his sadness by working harder on his scientific experiments.

In 1820, Hans Christian Oersted, a Danish scientist, discovered that an electric current can move the needle of a compass. Ampère heard about the discovery, and seven days later he was able to explain it by the use of mathematics. He also showed that two parallel wires carrying electric current attract or repel each other, depending on the direction of the currents. Ampère's work led to the invention of the *galvanometer*, which detects currents, and the *telegraph*, which transmits information by sending pulses of electric current along a wire.

The principles described by Ampère are used today in the operation of radio, television, electric motors, and other equipment. The unit of flow of an electric current was named the *ampere* (usually shortened to *amp*) to honor Ampère for his work.

▶ ▶ ▶ ▶ **FIND OUT MORE** ◀ ◀ ◀ ◀
Electricity; Magnet

AMPHETAMINE

SEE ADDICTION, DRUG, DRUG ABUSE

AMPHIBIAN

Animals that spend part of their lives in water and part on land are called *amphibians*. Usually, they hatch from eggs laid in streams or ponds. As adults, they move to land to live. The word amphibian comes from a Greek word that means "living a double life."

The animals in the class Amphibia are placed by scientists midway

◀ **An amoeba moves by first putting out a "false foot" or pseudopod. The rest of the animal follows behind.**

▲ **Ampère was a pioneer of electricity and magnetism.**

▲ **Millions of years ago, amphibians such as these developed on earth. They probably crawled out of the water to feed on land.**

The largest amphibian is the Japanese giant salamander which grows up to 5 feet (1.5 m) long. The largest salamander in the United States is the Hellbender, which can reach lengths of 3 feet (0.9 m). The smallest frog in the world can sit on a person's thumbnail.

between fishes and reptiles in the animal kingdom. They probably developed millions of years ago from fish that stayed out of water for longer and longer periods. The first amphibians were the forerunners of all backboned land animals. None of the early amphibians exists today. Most forms of amphibians died out altogether. Those that survived evolved into the frogs, toads, and salamanders we know today.

Although they breathe air, almost all amphibians must return to the water to lay their eggs. The young amphibians, called *larvae*, often tadpoles or pollywogs, hatch in the water. They breathe by means of gills like fish, and swim using their tails as paddles. As they grow, they go through a *metamorphosis*, or change. They usually lose their gills and tails, grow legs, and begin breathing with their lungs. Then, like their parents, they are able to live on land. Some salamanders breed on dry land, where they give birth to their young.

Amphibians usually have legs and a moist skin, which may be soft and smooth or rough and gritty. Unlike reptiles, amphibians do not have

scales on their skin, and their toes are without claws.

There are two main kinds of amphibians—those with tails as adults and those without. All amphibians have tails when they are babies. Some kinds, such as frogs, lose their tails as they grow, but others, such as salamanders, keep them. Salamanders have long bodies, tails, and short stubby legs. Some kinds of very primitive amphibians with tails but no legs are called *caecilians*. Caecilians spend their lives either in water or burrowing in warm, moist earth. They look like earthworms.

A toad has stubbier legs than a frog, and its body is usually wider and flatter. A frog has smooth skin. A toad has rough skin, which often feels lumpy to the touch because of glands that make it look warty.

◄ **Frogs and toads look similar. You can tell a frog (below) by its moist, shiny skin. A toad (left) has a dry, rougher skin. Also, frogs hop farther than toads.**

Amphibians have eyes similar to those of mammals. But they probably do not see very well. They have nostrils, but it is doubtful that they have a good sense of smell. They do not have visible ears, yet they do have eardrums—below and behind their eyes.

Most amphibians make their homes near freshwater ponds and lakes, or in damp places on land. Many amphibians hibernate during

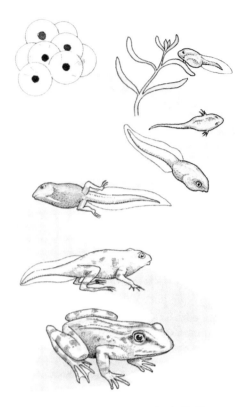

▲ **The life cycle of a frog: the jellylike eggs, or spawn, are laid in a pond and, after about five days, hatch into tadpoles; over the next few weeks or months, as the tadpoles grow, they gradually develop legs and their tails shrink; they also develop lungs instead of gills; they become adult frogs in about three years.**

the winter in cool climates. When an amphibian senses danger, it either stays still, blending in with its surroundings, or it runs away. Some amphibians have skin glands that produce an irritating, sometimes poisonous substance as a defense. If a hungry fish or some other animal bites off the tail of a salamander, the salamander grows a new tail. Regrowth of a body part, such as a tail, is called *regeneration*. Many amphibians are helpful to humans, because they eat insect pests.

▶▶▶▶ **FIND OUT MORE** ◀◀◀◀
Aquarium; Frogs and Toads; Metamorphosis; Reptile; Salamander; Terrarium; Vertebrate

LEARN BY DOING

You can keep one or two frog or toad tadpoles in a home aquarium. Put rocks and soil at one end of the aquarium and water from a pond at the other. Put the tadpole in the water. Feed it once each day with lettuce, watercress, or plants from the pond where you found it.

In a few weeks, the tail of the tadpole will begin to shrink. You will see its legs start to form. Lungs will take over from the gills. Soon the frog or toad will venture onto land. Write notes to record the animal's development. Then release the young frog or toad in the country or a park near the water where you found the tadpole. It can then grow and breed, so there will be more tadpoles next spring.

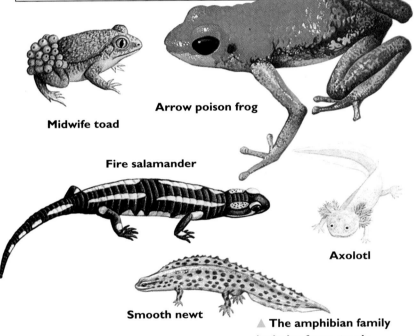

Midwife toad

Arrow poison frog

Fire salamander

Axolotl

Smooth newt

▼ **The spring salamander belongs to one of the seven salamander families that live in North America. It is generally good-natured but may defend itself by biting.**

▲ **The amphibian family includes frogs, toads, newts, and salamanders as well as the curious axolotl of Mexico, which keeps the feathery gills of its larval form as an adult.**

AMSTERDAM

In the city of Amsterdam, in the Netherlands (Holland), there are more than 50 canals and over 400 bridges. No wonder travelers who visit Amsterdam call it the "Venice of the North" for, like Venice, this is a city of canals. Amsterdam is a city built in, on, and around water. It stands on a dike, or dam, on the Amstel River. Even the Royal Palace rests on thousands of wooden piles placed there in 1650. The modern buildings in Amsterdam rest on strong concrete piles that go deep into the sandy soil.

▼ Amsterdam prospered in the 17th century because of overseas trade. These merchants' homes in the city were built at this time. The canal network is a feature of Amsterdam.

Amsterdam is the capital of the Netherlands, but government affairs are conducted in another city, The Hague. Amsterdam is a major European port and banking center. It is also a center of the diamond-cutting industry. Amsterdam was the home of the famous 17th-century artist Rembrandt van Rijn, commonly known as Rembrandt. Many of his paintings are owned by the city's Rijksmuseum.

Amsterdam became a city long before Columbus sailed for the New World. People still use buildings that date back to 1300. After the Netherlands won independence from Spain in the 1500s, Amsterdam became one of the great cities of Europe. In its early days, the city of New York was called New Amsterdam.

▶ ▶ ▶ ▶ **FIND OUT MORE** ◀ ◀ ◀ ◀
Netherlands; Rembrandt van Rijn

AMUNDSEN, ROALD (1872–1928)

The first person to reach the South Pole was Roald Amundsen, a Norwegian explorer. Amundsen was born in Borge, near Oslo, Norway. He attended the University of Christiania and then joined the Norwegian navy.

Amundsen made a three-year expedition to the Arctic beginning in 1903. He was the first to navigate the Northwest

▶ In 1911, Norway's Roald Amundsen was the first explorer to reach the South Pole. His race against Britain's Robert Scott was reported around the world.

Passage, a northern water route from the Atlantic to the Pacific. But Amundsen's greatest voyage began in 1910, at the other end of the Earth.

He intended to go to the North Pole, but he heard that Robert Peary had already reached it. So instead Amundsen headed to the South Pole in his ship, *Fram*. He learned that a British expedition, led by Robert F. Scott, was also on its way there.

Amundsen reached Antarctica in January, 1911. He and his men had to wait out the bitter cold, windy winter on the edge of the ice before they could head for the South Pole. In October (Antarctica's spring), they set out, with 52 well-trained dogs to pull their sledges. On the way to the Pole, they climbed glaciers, went around huge cracks in the ice, and survived freezing blizzards. Finally, on December 14, 1911, Amundsen placed the Norwegian flag at the South Pole. Scott and his men found the flag there when they reached the Pole a month after Amundsen's party.

Amundsen died in the Arctic, 17 years later. He disappeared while making an air search for another explorer, Umberto Nobile.

▶▶▶▶ **FIND OUT MORE** ◀◀◀◀
Antarctica; Arctic; North Pole; Northwest Passage; Scott, Robert F.

ANALGESIC

When you have a headache, fever, or a bad cold you might be given aspirin or some other pill to relieve the aches and pains. Your grandmother might need to take medicine to control her arthritis. Something that helps to stop or reduce pain is called an analgesic.

Analgesics vary greatly in strength. Mild analgesics can control a temporary pain like a headache. Most households have some in the medicine chest. Aspirin is the most common of these remedies. Some people prefer other mild, non-aspirin anal-

gesics, such as Tylenol, because aspirin, a type of acid, may upset their stomach.

Stronger analgesics are needed to help people with the constant pain of illnesses such as a fracture (broken bone) or cancer. Codeine and morphine are powerful analgesics.

Although scientists know that analgesics control pain, they cannot say exactly how these drugs work. Most analgesics work with the body's *nervous system,* which sends signals of pain to the brain. The medicines affect these signals and change the message that the brain receives.

There is little danger of becoming addicted to aspirin or other mild analgesics. But these drugs can cause serious illnesses and even death if the instructions are not followed.

Many of the more powerful analgesics are *narcotic,* or addictive. They control severe pain, but they can make people crave them. Too much of these drugs can also be fatal.

Because of the potential for abuse, narcotic analgesics can only be bought from a pharmacist, using a *prescription,* or order, from a doctor or dentist. Other analgesics can be bought "over the counter," but their instructions must be followed carefully.

▶▶▶▶ **FIND OUT MORE** ◀◀◀◀
Anesthetics; Drug; Drug Abuse; Narcotics

ANATOMY

Anatomy is the study of how living things—plants, animals, and people are built. The word comes from the Greek word, *anatome,* meaning "to cut up."

Dissecting, or cutting apart, dead human bodies was a crime in ancient times. In the 1st century A.D., Galen,

▼ Willow bark has been used to alleviate pain and fever for at least 2,000 years. Meadowsweet was also useful in reducing pain and fever.

White Willow

Meadowsweet

▲ Anatomy owes much to Vesalius, the first great anatomist. He made careful drawings, like the one above, of the human body.

► The ancient Egyptians farmed fields alongside the Nile. In this Egyptian tomb painting you can see farmers cutting wheat and carrying it to be threshed. The grain is being separated from the chaff by tossing it up into the air (the lighter chaff blows away while the heavier grain falls to the ground). Wheat harvesting was done twice a year.

a Greek doctor, dissected animals to study their parts. His writings on anatomy remained important until the 1400s. Andreas Vesalius, a Belgian doctor, wrote a famous book on anatomy in 1543. It was based on his dissections of dead human bodies.

There are several branches of anatomy. *Gross anatomy* is the study of large parts of the body. *Histology* is the study of tissue, and *cytology* is the study of cells. *Comparative anatomy* deals with differences in structure.

▶▶▶▶ **FIND OUT MORE** ◀◀◀◀
Biology; Human Body

ANCIENT CIVILIZATIONS

Many civilizations have grown and then disappeared in places all over the world. The ancient civilizations that most affected the development of the western world were those that formed around the Mediterranean Sea. The first was the Sumerian civilization, which existed more than 5,000 years ago, and the last was the Western Roman Empire, which fell in A.D. 476. The ancient civilizations of the Mediterranean included the

Egyptians, the Babylonians, the Persians, the Phoenicians, the Minoans, the Mycenaeans, and the Greeks.

There were other ancient and impressive civilizations in China, India, Africa, and North and South America. However, the contributions of these peoples to the way people of the Western World live today are not so easily traced.

Thousands of years ago, people everywhere lived in small groups, or tribes. Almost everyone in a group worked at hunting animals and gathering wild plants for food. Tribes roamed all over, searching for food. This *nomadic*, or wandering, life went on until some people discovered that they could plant seeds and raise crops. Then they *domesticated*, or tamed, animals, such as goats, sheep, and cattle to use for food, and raised other animals, such as donkeys, camels, and horses, as beasts of burden.

The first cities developed in areas that were especially good for farming. On a farm, so much food could be raised that not everyone had to work to provide the next meal. People worked as full-time priests, government officials, soldiers, craftsmen,

▼ An ancient Sumerian village probably looked much like this. The huts were made of marsh reeds, just like these in Iraq today.

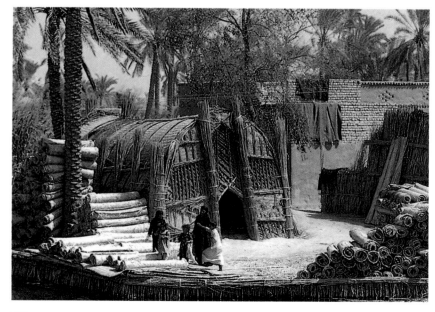

merchants, artists, and musicians. Life became very complex. Writing was developed to help people conduct the business of their cities.

The Gifts of Ancient Civilizations

WRITING. With the invention of writing, people could make lasting records of their laws, religions, folktales, poetry, and business deals. The Sumerians were the first people to develop word writing, more than 5,000 years ago. Before the Sumerians, if a writer wanted to say "9 cows," he had to draw 9 small pictures of cows. A Sumerian writer simply wrote the word-character for "cow" and the number-symbol for "9." This Sumerian writing is called *cuneiform* (wedge-shaped), because characters were scratched into soft clay tablets with a wedge-shaped stick, or reed.

About 3000 B.C., the Egyptians developed a writing system called *hieroglyphics,* or "sacred carving." Hieroglyphics were first chiseled into stone monuments, but later they were written with pen and ink. Like cuneiform, hieroglyphics was word writing, but the characters were different, because they were not made with a wedge-shaped stick. Both sys-

tems later added new characters for syllable sounds. Many hundreds of years later, people who lived on the eastern shores of the Mediterranean Sea invented the first alphabets.

MEDICINE AND SCIENCE. The Egyptians had highly skilled doctors who understood the human body. The Greeks, too, had good doctors. Hippocrates, a Greek doctor who lived 400 years before Christ, is called the "father of modern medicine." His ideas formed the basis of modern medicine, which developed in the 1800s. The Greeks also had many famous mathematicians and scientists, such as Euclid and Archimedes. The Mayans of Central America, whose empire lasted from about A.D. 300 to 900, were skilled astronomers and mathematicians.

LITERATURE. People continue to read and enjoy the literature of the ancient Greeks. Homer's epic poems, the *Iliad* and the *Odyssey,* are great literature as are the plays of Sophocles, Aeschylus, Euripides, and Aristophanes. From the Romans came the magnificent poetry of Ovid,

▼ **People in Mesopotamia used seals instead of signing letters. Seals were rolled across moist clay to make an impression. This one shows Darius the Great, the king of Persia, hunting lions.**

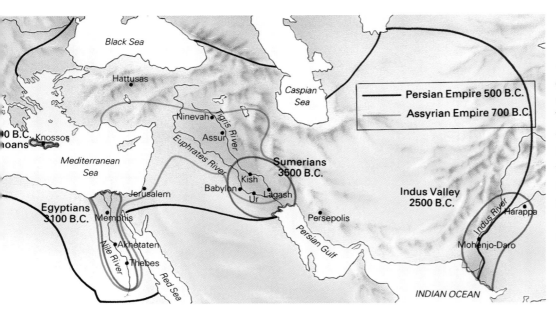

◄ **Some of the ancient civilizations and their major centers in the Old World. At the same time civilization also flourished in China, particularly under the Shang from about 1500 B.C. In America the Olmec civilization developed in Mexico from about 1200 B.C.**

ANCIENT CIVILIZATIONS

Location	Dates	Achievements	Cities	Why Did They Decline?
Sumerians lived between the Tigris and Euphrates rivers in what is now Iraq.	3500 B.C. to 2000 B.C.	First people to develop word writing, before 3000 B.C. Called *cuneiform* (wedge-shaped) writing, written on lumps of clay.	Kish, Lagash, Ur	Were conquered. But their art and architecture were so good that the invaders learned and copied from them. Babylonia later developed out of Sumeria.
Egyptians lived along the Nile River.	3100 B.C. to 525 B.C.	Built huge temples and large tombs, called pyramids, out of stone. Invented another form of word writing called *hieroglyphics*.	Memphis, Thebes, Akhetaton, Alexandria	Rebellions and invasions weakened the empire. Finally, conquered by the Kushites.
Minoans lived on the island of Crete near Greece.	3000 B.C. to 1100 B.C.	Made pottery and wall paintings full of bright, gay patterns. Built large outdoor theaters and loved to watch outdoor sports.	Knossos, Phaestos	Fell as Greece grew in power. Earthquakes may have speeded their end.
Indus Valley People lived in what is now Pakistan.	2500 B.C. to 1500 B.C.	Famous for their well-planned cities with neat blocks of buildings facing paved streets. Sewers ran under many of the streets. Fine craftsmen worked in the cities.	Harappa, Mohenjo-Daro	Vast floods damaged the cities. Invaders from the west probably conquered the people of the valley.
Hittites lived along the Halys River in what is now Turkey.	1900 B.C. to 1200 B.C.	Probably the first people to make things out of iron.	Hattusas	Allies of the Hittites rebelled. The Hittite city-states gradually lost power.
Babylonians lived between the Tigris and Euphrates rivers in what is now Iraq.	1900 B.C. to 538 B.C.	Great lawmakers. The Code of Hammurabi is one of the oldest known sets of written law. Even trade was governed by law. There were many scientists and mathematicians. They were the first people to count seconds and minutes by 60s.	Babylon	Conquered by the Persians in 538 B.C.
Phoenicians lived along eastern coast of the Mediterranean.	1100 B.C. to 842 B.C.	Invented an alphabet improved by the Greeks and used in the West today. Very skillful in making cloth and other goods. Traded in many parts of the world.	Byblos, Tyre, Sidon, Ugarit	Cities grew weaker as Assyria grew in power and took over most of the region.

▼ **The funeral procession of an Egyptian pharaoh in about 1567 to 1085 B.C.**

Chou were the people who established an empire along the western frontiers of the Shang State in China.

1027 B.C. to 256 B.C.

Iron tools replaced bronze. Literature and the visual arts reached great heights. Confucius and Lao-tzu, great philosophers and teachers, lived at this time.

Beijing, Chongqing

Generals and politicians argued with each other. China broke up into small, warring states.

Hebrews were originally nomadic. Lived at various times in what is now Israel and Jordan.

1000 B.C. to 587 B.C.

Created a great literature. Most important was the Old Testament of the Bible, the books of which were probably written between 900 B.C. and 150 B.C. King Solomon, a well-known king of Israel, built a great temple in Jerusalem.

Jerusalem, Hebron

The Babylonians conquered the Hebrews and destroyed the great temple in Jerusalem.

Assyrians lived along the Tigris River in what is now Iraq.

800 B.C. to 612 B.C.

Formed the first great army with iron weapons. This helped them win many battles.

Assur, Ninevah

Conquered by the Babylonians.

◀ **This coin shows the head of the Roman emperor Justinian who ruled the Eastern Roman Empire (now called the Byzantine Empire) from A.D. 450 to 527.**

Greeks lived in the southern part of what is now Greece.

800 B.C. to 197 B.C.

Built fine buildings and sculptures. Wrote great poetry and drama. Had many wise scientists and philosophers. Democracy began in Greece.

Athens, Sparta, Thebes, Corinth

The Roman Empire was gaining strength, taking away trade and turning farmers into soldiers. Rome finally conquered Greece.

Romans spread from the city of Rome west to England and east to Mesopotamia. At its height, included all lands around the Mediterranean.

735 B.C. to A.D. 476

Excellent administrators, first to control a vast area from a central place and still let cities govern themselves. Used their army to build bridges and roads to improve the lives of conquered peoples.

Rome, Pompeii, Constantinople

Civil war and political assassinations tore the Roman Empire apart. The empire split in half in A.D. 395. The western Romans became easy prey for invaders. The eastern empire continued until A.D. 1453.

▶ **The Phoenicians were famous for their glassware, such as this perfume bottle. They invented the method of glassblowing around 100 B.C.**

▶ **An impression from a Sumerian cylinder seal made about 5,000 years ago. Cylinder seals were used to identify property and sign business contracts.**

Kushites lived in Africa along the Nile River, south of Egypt. Expanded through much of Africa below Sahara desert.

725 B.C. to A.D. 350

The city of Meroe became a great, iron-making center. Made beautiful pottery, built pyramids, temples, and palaces. Developed a written language not yet deciphered.

Meroe Napata

Conquered by their neighbors, the Ethiopians.

Persians lived in an area from the Indus River to the Aegean Sea at the height of the empire.

700 B.C. to 331 B.C.

Built huge palaces of mud, brick, and stone. Beasts of legend appeared in their wall paintings and sculptures. Mail was delivered by "Pony Express."

Persepolis

The Persian Empire crumbled before the army of Alexander the Great in 331 B.C.

▶ Three great civilizations were centered around the Mediterranean. The Phoenicians were great sailors and traders. The Greeks colonized many coastal areas, taking their culture with them. But eventually both these civilizations were conquered by the Romans.

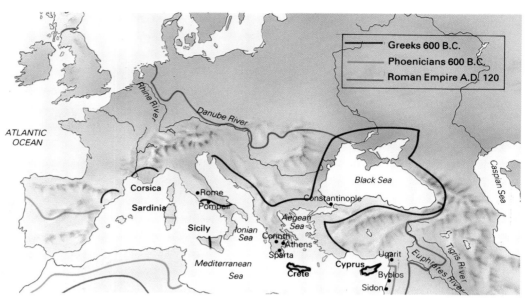

▼ Children in Ancient Egypt had many games and toys. Balls were made of leather or wood, and wooden toys were made with moving parts like this lion and wheeled horse.

Horace, and Virgil. The Bible, a book of sacred scriptures, is also great literature. It contains much ancient history and is the foundation of Jewish and Christian religious beliefs. Other world religions also produced ancient holy books.

PHILOSOPHY. Greek philosophers wondered about the nature of the universe. Others thought about conduct. The works of many Greek philosophers, including Socrates, Plato, and Aristotle, are still studied today. Chinese thinkers also won-dered about such questions. The writings of Confucius and Lao-tzu are still studied.

SCULPTURE, PAINTING, AND ARCHITECTURE. The ancient civilizations produced marvelous works of art. The Egyptians honored their pharaohs with enormous statues, tombs, and temples. Their stone pyramids were built to last for thousands of years, and to stand boldly against the desert sands. You can still see colorful scenes painted on the walls in many of their ornate tombs. On the Mediterranean island of Crete, the Minoan civilization lasted from about 3000 to 1100 B.C. The Minoans built huge palaces, painted, and made beautiful pottery. About the same time, the ancient Chinese made handsome bronze ritual vessels.

Ancient Greek temples are among the most magnificent buildings in history. The Greeks were also interested in the human body and produced some of the world's best sculpture of the human form. Roman sculptors copied many of their statues from the Greeks, but they also made some remarkably handsome portrait sculpture. The Romans built large, airy buildings with huge arches, vaults, and domed roofs. They also built countless bridges, roads, dams, and waterways. In Central America, the

---

LEARN BY DOING

Study the table on pages 156 and 157. It lists several of the famous ancient civilizations, what we remember them for, their famous cities, and reasons for the end of each civilization. Imagine you are a writer filling in this table 2,000 years from now. What would you say about our present civilization?

Mayan people built huge cities dominated by massive temples.

LAW AND DEMOCRACY. The idea that people should be ruled by a written *code* (set) of laws, and not by the whims of rulers, began in ancient times. One of the first and most famous codes of law came from Mesopotamia. King Hammurabi of Babylon, who lived almost 4,000 years ago, had laws carved on a stone column. The *Code of Hammurabi* may seem harsh to many today, but Babylonians who broke the law knew their crime and knew what their punishment would be.

The Greeks believed that the citizens should decide the laws. They called this form of government *democracy,* which means, "rule by the people." The Romans added to the Greek laws. Many laws of modern Western nations are based partly on these ancient codes, and some of the principles of modern democratic government are derived from the Greek and Roman systems.

Mysteries from the Past

Historians know that northern tribes invaded Rome in A.D. 476, thus ending the Western Roman Empire. Before this, Rome had taken over the Greeks' territory, and earlier still the Greeks had defeated the mighty Persian empire. But other ancient civilizations left almost no clue as to why they disappeared. For example, the Minoan empire crumbled after 1400 B.C., when all its towns and palaces burned. No one knows why.

Scientists called *archeologists* search the sites of ancient cities for walls, broken pieces of sculpture, pottery, cooking tools, and other clues to the lives of long-ago peoples. Scientists can measure very accurate-

▼ **Under the supervision of their king, Assyrian workers toil to bring materials for building a new palace. While slaves drag a huge statue of a winged, human-headed bull from the quarry, oarsmen in skin boats tow a raft along the Tigris.**

◄ **A painted drinking cup, showing a wounded soldier being bandaged. It was made in Athens in the 5th century B.C. Pottery, an important Athenian export, was traded all around the Mediterranean.**

Money was not used in ancient Egypt. Everyone was paid in goods, usually food. This food was taken from the farmers as a tax. Several times during the 20th Egyptian dynasty, the workmen building a tomb for the pharaoh were not paid their food on time. They went on strike. The men marched to the temple where supplies were kept and sat down outside calling for bread. They soon got what they wanted, because it was unthinkable that the pharaoh's tomb should not be finished.

▼ **The ruins of Pompeii, as they are today. This Roman town was buried by falling ash and lava when the volcano Vesuvius erupted in A.D. 79.**

ly when objects were made and used, so we can learn a surprising amount about the way people lived. Yet hundreds of mysteries and unanswered questions remain about each ancient civilization.

▶▶▶▶ **FIND OUT MORE** ◀◀◀◀

Architecture see Abu Simbel; Acropolis; Archeology; Great Wall of China; Parthenon; Pyramid; Seven Wonders of the World; Stonehenge

Art see Art History; Greek Art; Oriental Art; Roman Art; Sphinx

Leaders of Long Ago see Alexander The Great; Caesar, Julius; Cleopatra; Hannibal; Nero; Spartacus; Xerxes I

The Peoples see Assyria; Babylonia; Byzantine Empire; Carthage; Egypt, Ancient; Etruscan; Greece, Ancient; Jewish History; Macedonia; Maya; Mesopotamia; Palestine; Persia; Phoenicia; Pompeii; Rome, Ancient; Sumer

Philosophy and Religion see Aristotle; Buddhism; Christianity; Confucius; Hinduism; Islam; Judaism; Philosophy; Plato; Religion; Socrates

Written Language see Alphabet; Hieroglyphics; Rosetta Stone; Written Language

QUIZ

1. Who first invented the alphabet we use today? Who improved upon it?

2. Which island was inhabited by the Minoan civilization?

3. The oath all doctors take before they start practicing medicine is named for the Greek "father of modern medicine." What is it called?

4. Which were developed first: iron tools, or bronze?

(Answers on page 256)

ANDERSEN, HANS CHRISTIAN (1805–1875)

Once upon a time, in Denmark, a boy dreamed and played with his puppets. The neighborhood children laughed at him, and adults said he was a fool. But he grew up to become one of the most famous and best-loved writers of all time. He was Hans Christian Andersen.

Andersen was born in the village of Odense. His father was a shoemaker, and his mother washed clothes to earn money. His father would read to the boy on cold winter evenings, sometimes from *The Arabian Nights*. His father died when Andersen was 11 years old. Hans had to give up school. He went to Copenhagen three years later, with only a little money from his savings. He was determined to become famous.

He tried very hard to be an actor, singer, or dancer in Copenhagen, but he almost starved. Then a director of the Royal Theater befriended him. Andersen was given a scholarship so he could finish his education. Going back to school was difficult for him, because he was older than the other students who made fun of him.

Andersen's first fairy tales were published in 1835. In all, he wrote 168 stories. He was sensitive and kind, and he fell in love three times, but he never married. His fairy tales brought him the fame for which he had yearned, and he went on writing them until 1872. He also wrote novels, plays, and poems.

The stories that Hans Christian Andersen wrote are not just for children. They are for people of all ages, in all times. "The Little Mermaid" is one of the saddest and also one of the most loved of his stories. "The Emperor's New Clothes" is a happier tale, and so are "The Princess and the Pea," and "The Ugly Duckling." Most of these tales have a moral, or lesson. Things that Andersen loved as a child appear in his stories. His mother's garden is the garden of "The Snow Queen." His grandmother told him the tale that became "The Tinderbox."

The fairy tales of Hans Christian Andersen have been translated into over 80 languages. They have been made into movies, plays, ballets, and puppet shows. In Copenhagen harbor stands a statue, *The Little Mermaid,* the people of Denmark's memorial to Hans Andersen, who once said, "Life is the most wonderful fairy tale of all."

▶▶▶▶ **FIND OUT MORE** ◀◀◀◀
Fairy Tale

▲ The distinguished singer Marian Anderson, who was also made a delegate to the United Nations.

ANDERSON, MARIAN (1902–1993)

Marian Anderson was 6 years old when she first sang in public, in the choir of the Union Baptist Church in Philadelphia, her home city. She grew up to became one of the world's greatest singers.

Marian Anderson's parents were poor. Her church helped to pay for singing lessons. After years of voice training, she entered a contest to sing with the New York Philharmonic Orchestra and won first place out of 300 contestants.

She went to Europe, where her concerts thrilled many people. But she was not allowed to sing in

◀ An illustration from *The Princess and the Pea,* one of Hans Christian Andersen's best-loved stories. In it the test of a real princess is whether or not she can feel a pea through 20 mattresses and 20 quilts.

Constitution Hall in Washington, D.C., in 1939, because she was black. First Lady Eleanor Roosevelt invited her to sing on the steps of the Lincoln Memorial instead. Anderson gave a memorable, free concert there on Easter Sunday 1939.

In 1955, Marian Anderson became the first black person to sing with the Metropolitan Opera Company in New York. She later sang at the White House. Her rich-textured contralto voice was at its best singing Negro Spirituals. She picked the title of one spiritual, "My Lord, What a Morning," as the title of her autobiography. She received many honors, including the Spingarn Medal and the Presidential Medal of Freedom.

▶▶▶▶ **FIND OUT MORE** ◀◀◀◀
Singing

ANDES MOUNTAINS

The Andes curve like a vast wall down the western side of South America. They form the longest mountain chain in the world: about 5,500 miles (8,900 km). Only the Himalaya Mountains of Asia rise higher. Forty-two Andean peaks are taller than Mount McKinley, North America's tallest mountain. The highest peak in the Andes and in the Western Hemisphere is Aconcagua, in Argentina. It rises to a height of 22,834 feet (6,960 m).

Fingers of the Andes almost touch the Caribbean Sea in the north. Three separate ranges come together in Colombia. The Andes then continue south through Ecuador and Peru, become widest in Bolivia and border Chile on the way to disappearing into the ocean at the tip of South America. Some evidence shows the range continues in Antarctica. (See the map with the article on SOUTH AMERICA.)

The Andes region is one of fire and ice. Many active volcanoes show that these mountains are still being formed. Earthquakes sometimes shake the area. Great glaciers, warmed by the sun, can slide down valleys.

Spanish explorers looked for the Incas' source of gold in the Andes in the 1500s. Many other valuable mineral ores have been found and mined there in modern times. Today Andean people still live simply, high up in these mountains.

▶▶▶▶ **FIND OUT MORE** ◀◀◀◀
Inca; Mountain; South America

ANDORRA

The tiny country of Andorra lies high in the Pyrenees Mountains between France and Spain. Catalan, which is somewhat like both French and Spanish, is the language of Andorra.

Fall is a busy season in Andorra, because the farmers must get ready for a long, hard winter. Farmers grow tobacco and potatoes, and raise sheep and cattle. The capital city, Andorra la Vella, is a colorful sight, with ancient stone houses, shops, and modern hotels.

Tourism has become an important industry. Thousands of tourists arrive to look at the beautiful countryside

▼ **The Andes Mountains, the second highest range in the world, were the last stronghold of the Incas. The Inca mountain fortress at Machu Picchu shown here remained undiscovered by Europeans until 1911.**

and also to buy inexpensive goods. There is no sales tax in Andorra. Skiing attracts many visitors. On some slopes the snow lasts until April.

Charlemagne, emperor of the Holy Roman Empire, gave this tiny country its independence in the 700s, as a reward to the Andorrans for helping him in battle. An arrangement was made in 1278 for two co-princes to rule Andorra. On March 14, 1993, the co-princes, the Bishop of Urgel in Spain and the President of France, François Mitterrand, signed off on a new constitution that makes the tiny country Europe's newest sovereign state. This was done after the country's 9,123 voters opted overwhelmingly for independence.

Pic de Coma Pedrosa 9,652 ft. 2,942 m

© 1994 GeoSystems, an R.R. Donnelley & Sons Company

▶ ▶ ▶ ▶ **FIND OUT MORE** ◀ ◀ ◀ ◀
Charlemagne; Europe; Spain

▶ **Andorra la Vella, the capital of the tiny country of Andorra, sits beneath the rocky, but beautiful, Pyrenees Mountains. The town is a popular destination for tourists, who provide the country's chief source of income.**

ANDROMEDA

The story of Andromeda is one of the myths of ancient Greece. Andromeda was the daughter of Cepheus and Cassiopeia, king and queen of Ethiopia.

Cassiopeia was very vain. She boasted that Andromeda was as beautiful as the nymphs of Poseidon, god of the sea. Her boasting made Poseidon very angry, so he sent a horrible sea monster to attack Ethiopia. To save their kingdom, the king and queen chained Andromeda to a rock and left her for the monster.

The hero Perseus saw her and instantly fell in love with her. He killed the monster, carried off Andromeda and married her. Hercules was one of the descendants of Andromeda and Perseus. After Andromeda's death, the gods turned Andromeda into a constellation of stars in the sky. At the heart of the Andromeda constellation shines a beautiful galaxy.

▶ ▶ ▶ ▶ **FIND OUT MORE** ◀ ◀ ◀ ◀
Gods And Goddesses; Mythology; Perseus

ANDORRA

Capital city
Andorra la Vella
(15,700 people)

Area
175 square miles
(435 sq. km)

Population
51,000 people

Government
Co-principality

Main products
Tourism, tobacco products

Unit of money
French franc and Spanish peseta

Official language
Catalan (Spanish and French are also spoken)

ANEMIA

Anemia is a blood problem that leaves people feeling weak or dizzy. It is caused when the number of red blood cells falls below normal. These cells carry oxygen to muscles in all parts of the body in order to create energy.

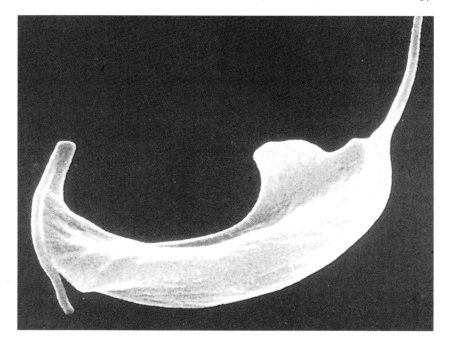

▲ Sickle cell anemia is an inherited blood disease that mostly affects black people and also people from Mediterranean countries. It is so named because some of the sufferer's red blood cells, instead of being round, are twisted into sickle shapes.

Before anesthetics were commonly used in operations, circus acts entertained American audiences with a "grand exhibition of laughing gas." The gas was guaranteed to make those who inhaled it "laugh, sing, dance, or fight."

When not enough oxygen reaches the muscles, a person loses energy. We say that he or she is *anemic.*

Eating certain foods can help prevent anemia. Foods containing iron, for example, help *bone marrow* produce more red blood cells. This is the soft tissue inside your bones that makes billions of new red blood cells every hour. Eggs, red meat, cereals, and green vegetables contain iron.

Prolonged bleeding can sometimes lead to anemia. Or anemia can be a symptom of a disease. *Leukemia* can prevent the bone marrow from making red blood cells. *Sickle cell anemia* distorts the body's *hemoglobin,* the part of the red blood cell that enables it to carry oxygen. This disease is inherited, and African-Americans are most at risk.

▶ ▶ ▶ ▶ **FIND OUT MORE** ◀ ◀ ◀ ◀
Blood; Bone

ANESTHETICS

Doctors sometimes need to perform a procedure or an operation, which may hurt a patient. They give the patient a drug called an *anesthetic,* which keeps the patient from feeling pain. "Anesthetic" comes from two Greek words meaning "without feeling." A *general* anesthetic makes a patient unconscious. A *local* anesthetic stops all feeling in one part of the patient's body. A dentist, for example, injects a local anesthetic into the patient's gums so he or she does not feel any pain while a tooth is being filled or pulled.

Before the discovery of modern anesthetics, patients drank alcohol or took drugs to make them sleepy before operations. Modern anesthetics weren't discovered until the 1800s.

Dr. Crawford Williamson Long of Jefferson, Georgia, first used a chemical called *ether* as an anesthetic in

▲ The Morton inhaler was a device used to give ether as an anesthetic.

December 1842. Three months later he used it when he removed a tumor from a patient's neck. Records show he charged 25 cents for the ether.

In 1844, a Connecticut dentist named Horace Wells had patients sniff *nitrous oxide* before a tooth was pulled. This mild anesthetic, which is still in use, does not put a person completely to sleep. It is called "laughing gas," because it makes

people feel happy and giggly while feeling no pain.

Meanwhile, a Boston dentist, Dr. William Morton, was also trying ether. He persuaded a surgeon, Dr. John Warren, to let him give a patient some ether to breathe before an operation in 1846. Dr. Warren was doubtful, but the patient went quietly to sleep. The astonished Dr. Warren exclaimed to a group of doctors who were watching, "Gentlemen, this is no humbug!"

Dr. James Young Simpson, a Scotsman, gave an anesthetic called *chloroform* to a woman to breathe just before she gave birth to a baby in 1847. In 1853, Queen Victoria of Britain asked for chloroform when she gave birth to her seventh child. Anesthetics became popular after that.

When people have an operation today, they can remain safely unconscious all through it. The human body feels pain through the nerves. General anesthetics work on the central nervous system and prevent the sensation of pain being recognized by the brain.

Patients may be given some medication to relax them before an operation. Then an *intravenous* (into a vein) injection of an anesthetic makes the patient lose consciousness. An *anesthesiologist* (a doctor who gives anesthetics) continues to give anesthetic gas to keep the patient unconscious until the surgeon has finished the operation.

▶▶▶▶ **FIND OUT MORE** ◀◀◀◀
Drug; Drug Abuse; Medicine; Nervous System; Surgery

⚙ ANGLE

Two straight lines meet at a point to form an angle. The point where the lines meet is called the *vertex* of the angle. If the lines make a square corner, they form a *right angle*. A street corner is often a right angle. An angle smaller than a right angle is called *acute*. An angle larger than a right angle is called *obtuse*. The size of an angle is measured in units called *degrees*. A full circle contains 360 degrees. The symbol ° stands for degrees.

▶▶▶▶ **FIND OUT MORE** ◀◀◀◀
Geometry

◀ **Dr. William Morton of Boston began using ether as an anesthetic in 1846. He tried to keep anesthesia with ether his exclusive property and spent most of the rest of his life in legal action.**

It is sometimes difficult to make an exact right angle. An easy way is to fold a piece of paper in half and then fold it a second time along the crease. You how have a perfect right angle.

LEARN BY DOING

Draw the face of a clock. It is a circle, so it has 360°. Attach hands to the clock using a straight pin and two long strips of paper. Point one hand at 12 and the other at 3. The hands form a right angle of 90° (one-fourth of 360°). Move the hand from 3 to 6. This does not look like an angle. But it is called a straight angle, and it contains 180°. Now move the hand from 6 to 8. Is this angle obtuse? How many degrees are there in this angle? If you are not sure, here is a clue—there are 30° between each five minutes on the clock face. Now try to form an angle that has 150°.

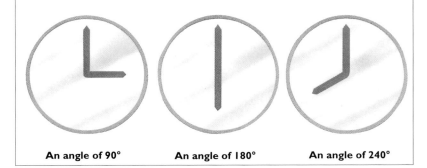

An angle of 90°   An angle of 180°   An angle of 240°

▼ **Most of the Anglo-Saxon invaders were farmers looking for new land. Here Anglo-Saxon farmworkers are harvesting wheat.**

ANGLO-SAXONS

Anglo-Saxon peoples from northern Europe invaded Britain over 1,500 years ago. They included Angles, Saxons, and Jutes, and they began to settle in Britain after its Roman rulers had left in the 5th century. The invad-

ing people drove the native Britons westward, and created their own kingdoms, which included Northumbria, Mercia, and Wessex. The most famous king of Wessex was Alfred the Great. The Anglo-Saxons gave the name *Englalond* (England) to their new land and ruled there until King Harold was defeated in the Norman Conquest of 1066.

▶ ▶ ▶ ▶ **FIND OUT MORE** ◀ ◀ ◀ ◀
Alfred The Great; English History; English Language

ANGLO

The country that today is the Republic of Angola was inhabited by African Bushmen and Bantu tribes until a Portuguese navigator, Diogo Cão, claimed the region for Portugal in 1482. The Portuguese developed the slave trade in the 16th century. For a brief time, 1641 to 1648, the Dutch took control of the region.

In the 1800s, Portugal tried unsuccessfully to gain territory in Africa's interior. Portugal hoped to connect Angola, then known as Portuguese West Africa, with another colony, Mozambique, known as Portuguese East Africa. Britain, however, forced Portugal out of the interior.

About 400,000 Portuguese settlers emigrated to Angola during the first half of the 20th century. They developed industries and hydroelectric power. Oil was discovered near Luanda, the capital, in 1955.

The black Angolans rebelled against the repressive Portuguese rule. Fighting broke out in 1960 and Portugal rushed in troops. A struggle for independence began. In 1972, Portugal changed Angola from an overseas province to an *autonomous*, or self-governing, state and in 1975, granted it full independence.

A fierce struggle for supremacy was waged among rival factions, with the Popular Movement (MPLA) gaining control of the government in 1976. The National Union (UNITA) resisted this takeover, fighting a civil war through the 1980s, with Cuban and South African troops involved. After an agreement in 1988, foreign troops started to withdraw slowly. In 1991, a peace pact was signed, which included an agreement to hold multi-party elections in 1992.

ANGOLA

Capital city
Luanda (1,134,000 people)

Area
481,354 square miles (1,246,700 sq. km)

Population
10,002,000 people

Government
Republic

Main products
Coffee, diamonds, oil

Unit of money
Kwanza

Official language
Portuguese

© 1994 GeoSystems, an R.R. Donnelley & Sons Company

Angola's land rises sharply beyond the narrow coastal plain, into a high plateau of forests and grasslands. The country has more than 900 miles (1,440 km) of coastline and many rivers. The climate is suitable for growing coffee, cotton, corn, sugar, and sisal. Mines in Angola produce diamonds, iron, and copper. Oil is an important export. Angola's industries include cereal mills, fish and palm oil processing plants, and foundries.

▶ ▶ ▶ ▶ **FIND OUT MORE** ◀ ◀ ◀ ◀
Africa; Portugal

▼ **Angola's capital is the seaport city of Luanda on the South Atlantic Ocean.**

ANIMAL

An animal is any living thing that is not a plant. The biggest difference between animals and plants is in the way they get their food. Animals eat plants or other animals. Most plants make their food out of substances taken in through their roots or leaves. Also most animals are able to move around, whereas most plants cannot.

There are some animals that look more like plants than animals. For example, the sea cucumber has no head or tail. Its body looks like a cucumber. The sea cucumber is only one of about a million different kinds of animals in the world. No one knows exactly how many there are; hundreds of new kinds are discovered every year.

All animals have certain things in common. They are all made of cells that are different from plant cells. They all can move, even if only for a part of their lives. And they all must take in food as a source of energy.

All living things are made up of tiny building blocks of living matter called *cells*. The cells of an animal have a baglike outer covering, called a *membrane*. The cell is soft, like a tiny balloon full of juice. It is in the cell that the activities that mean "life" happen. A cell takes in food, water, and oxygen, uses them to produce energy, and then gives off waste products. An animal can consist of a single cell

INVERTEBRATES

Butterfly (insect)

Jellyfish (coelenterate)

VERTEBRATES

Brown trout (fish)

Turtle (reptile)

River kingfisher (bird)

Chimpanzee (mammal)

Rhinoceros (mammal)

▶ **A mountain lion or puma, a big cat of North America, poised to pounce on its prey.**

that does all these things. An amoeba, for example, is a one-celled animal that lives in ponds. More complicated animals are made of larger numbers of cells. Many millions of cells working together make up the human animal.

The pressure of the atmosphere on Earth could flatten animal cells. But animals have adapted to certain ways of living or certain forms that prevent their being squashed. For example, one-celled animals always live in water, which helps the cell hold its shape. The water may be a pond, an ocean, or the fluid in a bigger animal's body. Other animals have developed outside coverings like

as mammals and birds, can see, hear, smell, feel, and taste. They have nervous systems that allow them to sense what is happening, then react quickly.

Animals have to *eat* in order to get energy to live. Plants produce their own food, using energy directly from the sun. Animals get the sun's energy indirectly by eating plants or by eating other animals that have eaten plants. Every animal has adapted to its own way of getting its share of the sun's energy. This is one reason for the fantastic variety of animal life.

▲ **Two male Ugandan kobs (a sort of antelope) fight to defend their territories.**

shells or inside supports such as bones that protect and shape them. The hard shell on a beetle is an outside protection, as is the "skin," called *cuticle*, of an earthworm. The skeleton of a bird or fish is a bony support inside the body.

At some time in its life, every animal is able to move its body. This is called *locomotion*. Most animals move all their lives. A sponge has a swimming "childhood," but spends its adult life attached to a rock.

Part of being able to move is the ability to react to what is happening around you. Simple, one-celled animals react to food by moving toward it and react to danger by moving away. Higher forms of animals, such

The koala is perhaps the most fussy eater of all the animals. It lives only on the leaves of eucalyptus trees—and only on the leaves of five out of the 350 species of eucalyptus at that!

▼ **The koala of Australia is sometimes called a "bear," but it is not a true bear at all. It is a marsupial and has a pouch in which the mother carries her young. Koala young remain in the pouch for at least six months after birth.**

ANIMAL DEFENSES

An animal needs to protect itself
from its enemies. If its defenses are
not good enough, it will not survive.
Every creature has some kind of
defense. The elephant has enormous
size and strength. A deer has speed.
An armadillo has an armor of thick,
horny plates. A cat has claws. A butterfly flies in a zigzag way, making it
difficult to catch.

At the first sign of danger, most
animals try to escape. For some animals, this means running away as
fast as they can. Antelopes, gazelles,
and many other mammals that live
in open country depend on speed. So
do many fish, insects, and birds.

Many animals escape by hiding.
The brightly colored little fish
around coral reefs are an example.
Each fish vanishes into its own hole
in the coral when trouble comes.
Some small land animals try to keep
their enemies from seeing them by
holding perfectly still in the tall grasses or bushes. Rabbits have been
known to "freeze" in this way for
half an hour or more.

Some animals are able to hide
from their enemies because they
match their surroundings. For
example, an insect called the walk-
ingstick lives in trees and looks
almost exactly like a small brown
twig. Because of this, it is practically

▼ **To ward off enemies the
hedgehog tucks in its head
and legs, forming a ball of
spines that few predators
can penetrate.**

invisible to its enemies. The color of
the skin or coat of desert animals,
such as the horned toad and the
desert rat, matches the sandy color of
the desert.

Some fish can change their color
to match different backgrounds. The
flounder, for example, will turn a
grayish-brown color if it is close to a
sandy area under the water. Its back
will even show little speckles that
look like grains of sand. Other creatures change color when the seasons
change. In winter, the Arctic fox and
the weasel, a small animal that looks
like a mink, change from brown to

If a worm is cut into
pieces, each piece will
form a complete new
worm. More amazing
is that if a worm is
"trained" to find its way
through a maze, then cut
in half and allowed to
regrow, both new worms
will remember their way
through the maze.

▲ In danger an armadillo rolls into a well-protected ball. The pangolin from Asia and Africa and some insects can do this too.

Summer coat

▼ A hognose snake flops down "dead" when threatened. This confuses some predators, who then give up the hunt.

pure white, so they can hardly be seen against the snow.

Special armor is a way of hiding for some creatures. Certain armadillos are covered with thick plates. When they roll themselves into tight balls, enemies cannot get at their soft flesh. Turtles and tortoises have hard shells to guard their tender bodies. They pull their heads and legs quickly into the safety of their shells. Clams, oysters, and similar sea creatures have shells that snap shut.

▼ One way to avoid being attacked is to avoid being seen in the first place. This can be done by camouflage. Some hares have a brown summer coat. In the autumn this molts and the hare grows white fur for camouflage in snow and ice.

Winter coat

Many animals have special ways to discourage attackers. Some play a game of "make believe" to fool their enemies. The hognose snake, a harmless, nonpoisonous creature, puts on a big show to scare off a would-be attacker. First it rears up and hisses, pretending to be ready to strike. If this does not succeed, the snake suddenly collapses and begins to twitch and roll

about, as if in agony. Then it flops on its back, looking as if it is dead.

Other beasts drive away their enemies with unpleasant smells, or even with smoke screens. When a skunk is alarmed, special glands near its tail shoot off a spray with a terrible odor. Stink bugs can release foul-smelling gases to drive away birds. If trapped, most animals will fight, using whatever weapons they have—horns, hoofs, claws, teeth, or stingers.

▶ ▶ ▶ ▶ **FIND OUT MORE** ◀ ◀ ◀ ◀

Animal Movement; Claws and Nails; Horns and Antlers; Protective Coloring; Teeth

ANIMAL DISTRIBUTION

Animals are found in every part of the earth, both on land and in water. The world's oceans are filled with saltwater fish, shellfish, octopuses, sea mammals, and numerous other creatures. The freshwater rivers, lakes, and ponds are populated by similar kinds of animals. Land animals, including birds, are found on all continents and in all cities. Humans are probably the only land animals that can survive on any continent and in almost any climate. Other kinds of animals are suited only for certain kinds of living places.

Places of Cold and Heat
The Antarctic, around the South Pole, is so icy and barren that people cannot live there for long. But penguins, seals, and whales are especially suited for polar life. They have heavy layers of fat under their skin to keep them warm, and they feed on the *plankton* (microscopic animal and plant life) and fish that abound in the Antarctic waters.

In the Arctic, around the North Pole, the climate is not quite so harsh, but it is still cold and snowy much of the year. Many of the

LEARN BY DOING

Use this encyclopedia to help make a list of other animals and their defenses. People too had to defend themselves for thousands of years without the kinds of weapons available today. Yet they survived. What ways might early people have used to defend themselves?

animals there, such as polar bears, Arctic foxes, lemmings, reindeer, and ermine, need thick coats of fur during the coldest months. The fur on some of these animals turns white in winter as protective coloring.

High mountains have living conditions similar to polar regions. So the animals of cold mountaintops also have heavy coats. Many of them—including the bighorn sheep of North America and the ibex, a wild goat of Asia—are also good at climbing the rocky cliffs.

Places In Between

Most animals, however, do not need to cope with such extremes of heat and cold. The forests, jungles, and open grasslands of *temperate* (in between) climates provide the right living conditions for many, many animals.

Some woodlands are *coniferous forests,* made up of cone-bearing trees such as pines or firs. A coniferous forest is often called a *taiga.* A taiga, found mainly in northern regions, provides homes for bears, moose, squirrels, woodpeckers, deer, beavers, and other animals. Many feed on the

Marco Polo, the Venetian explorer who spent 17 years at the court of Kublai Khan in China in the late 1200s, reported that the Great Khan had a collection of leopards, lynxes, tigers, and other animals. They were mostly used for hunting.

WHERE ANIMALS LIVE

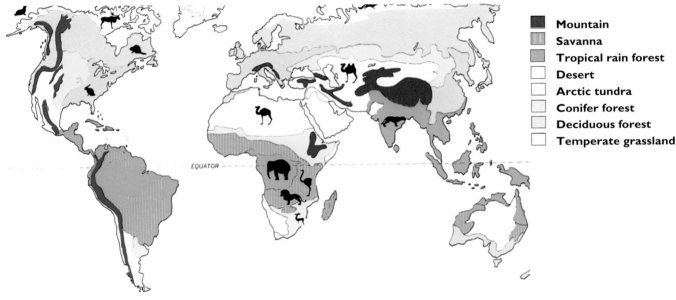

Mountain
Savanna
Tropical rain forest
Desert
Arctic tundra
Conifer forest
Deciduous forest
Temperate grassland

Animals living in deserts in Africa, Asia, North America, and Australia often have certain traits in common. Desert regions are very dry, and usually very hot. Many desert creatures are able to go for long periods without water. The kangaroo rat and the pocket mouse never drink water. They get enough water from the seeds and the plants that they eat. The dromedary, or one-humped camel, lives for long periods of time in the desert, where few plants grow. When it cannot get enough plant food, the animal's body uses the fat stored in its hump. Other desert animals include scorpions, jackrabbits, owls, lizards, and snakes. Some come out only at night, when it is cool.

nuts, berries, branches, and cones of such forests. Most coniferous forests stay green all year long.

Another kind of woodland is the *deciduous forest,* named from two Latin words that mean "to fall off." The broad leaves of deciduous trees fall off in autumn, and new leaves grow in the spring. Animals such as the cottontail rabbit, raccoon, chipmunk, opossum, and flying squirrel that live in these forests are able to survive in winter when food is scarce. Some of them store food for the cold months, and some sleep away the winter in hibernation.

Creatures that live in *tropical rain forests* and *jungles* are used to the heat and heavy rainfall there. In such

▲ **Many animals such as zebras, antelopes and wildebeest, graze together on the vast, open grasslands of the African Savanna.**

lation includes the maned wolf and the puma. Some unusual animals, such as the kangaroo, emu, and wombat, live in Australian savannas.

Many animals *migrate,* or move from one region to another, during certain seasons. Each year, North American robins, wild geese, and many songbirds escape the cold of winter by flying south to Florida or Mexico. In northern Europe, numerous animals make their way from Scandinavian countries to winter in warmer Africa.

▶▶▶▶ **FIND OUT MORE** ◀◀◀◀

Animal Homes; Ecology; Hibernation; Marine Life; Migration; Plant Distribution; Polar Life; Pond Life

ANIMAL FAMILIES

forests in Africa, there are elephants, hippopotamuses, chimpanzees, and crocodiles. Tigers, pythons, and gibbons live in the rain forests of Asia. In Latin American rain forests, you can find macaws, iguanas, toucans, jaguars, armadillos, and woolly monkeys.

Many animals live where there are few trees, or none at all. *Temperate grasslands* are flat, treeless plains in temperate, or mild, climates. In eastern Europe and parts of Asia, such lands are called *steppes.* They are somewhat arid, or dry, and have short grass. The Bactrian, or two-humped, camel is found in the steppes. In North America, the grasslands are called *prairies.* They have long grasses and are not as dry as the steppes. Pronghorns, prairie dogs, and coyotes are typical prairie beasts.

Savannas are grasslands found in tropical and subtropical regions. Some of the best-known savanna animals are those of Africa: lions, giraffes, vultures, leopards, zebras, rhinoceroses, and ostriches. In South America, the grassland animal popu-

Many animals work hard to raise their families. They give their young food, homes, and protection, and teach them how to take care of themselves. Other animals do not need to take care of their families at all.

Families are not important to most reptiles, amphibians, fish, and insects. Frogs, turtles, and most snakes lay eggs and leave them to hatch by themselves. The babies do not need parents, because they know how to care for themselves as soon as they hatch. Such knowledge is called *instinct.*

Most baby fish swim away by themselves after birth or after hatching. However, a few kinds of fish watch their eggs and even build nests. One fish, the stickleback, lives in both freshwater and salt water. It builds an igloo-shaped nest on the ocean floor or in a stream. The female lays her eggs inside the nest, and the male guards them until the young hatch.

Most insects lay their eggs and go away, never to return to them. But ants and bees build special nurseries for their young. Great numbers of worker ants or bees feed the young grubs, called *larvae,* until they become adults.

Families are important to birds and mammals, because their young cannot survive alone. They need care and they must learn how to fend for themselves. Often both mother and father share the work. For example, a mother wolf seeks out a hidden spot, such as a cave, where she gives birth to her cubs. The father stands guard. Like all mammals, the mother feeds the tiny cubs with milk from her own body. The father helps to hunt food for them as they get older. Both parents teach the young how to hunt when the cubs are old enough.

Mothers alone care for the young of many other mammals. Fathers are not really needed. For example, deer do not eat meat, so the parents do not have to hunt food for the fawns. The mother deer, or *doe,* feeds them milk until they can eat plants.

Other mammal mothers have special problems with their young. Pouched mammals, or *marsupials,* such as kangaroos, are born so tiny and helpless that the young have to spend weeks or months in a pouch on the mother's abdomen. Even when a baby kangaroo can hop about on its own, it still returns to the pouch to escape danger.

Most birds build nests for their eggs. The parents often take turns sitting on the eggs to incubate them until the chicks hatch. The parents share the work of finding food to feed the chicks. In time, they coax the

▼ **Gorillas are the largest of the apes. They live in troops of one or more adult males and several females. Troops are led by an old male. Like monkeys and humans, gorillas belong to the mammal order of primates.**

▼ **A kangaroo carries its baby inside a pouch. A baby kangaroo lives in its mother's pouch for weeks or even months before it begins to hop about.**

SOME ANIMAL FAMILIES

	Male name	Female name	Baby name	Group name
Kangaroo	Buck or Boomer	Doe or Flyer	Joey	Troop, Mob, or Herd
Cat	Tom	Puss	Kitten	Clowder
Dog	Dog	Bitch	Pup	Kennel or Pack
Horse	Stallion	Mare	Foal (m or f) Colt (m) Filly (f)	Herd
Deer	Stag or Buck	Doe	Fawn	Herd
Hog	Boar	Sow	Piglet	Drove
Rabbit	Buck	Doe	Kit	Warren
Lion	Lion	Lioness	Cub	Pride
Chicken	Rooster or Cock	Hen	Chick	Flock
Fox	Fox	Vixen	Kit or Cub	Skulk
Swan	Cob	Pen	Cygnet	Flock
Whale	Bull	Cow	Calf	Herd or School

babies out for their first flying lesson.

But some birds do not build nests at all. The female emperor penguin lays a single egg on frozen snow. The male penguin immediately puts the egg on top of his feet where it is kept warm by his body. Groups of father penguins stay with the eggs for two months while the mothers swim out to sea to catch fish. When the eggs hatch, the mothers return. They begin months of feeding and protecting that allow the chicks to grow strong and independent.

▶▶▶▶ **FIND OUT MORE** ◀◀◀◀
Animal; Animal Homes; Ant; Bee; Bird;
Child Care; Mammal; Reproduction

ANIMAL HOMES

The beaver is one of the best-known animal home makers. Beavers build a *lodge* of branches and mud next to a riverbank, or even in the center of a pond. The entrance is always underwater, but the rooms inside are above the water. A lodge may house a single beaver family or be large enough for several families. Nearby, under the water, the beavers store a food supply of bark and other plants.

Like the beaver, other animals find or build homes that are specially suited for their way of life. Many birds make nests in high places, such as trees, chimneys, and barn roofs. Large birds, such as eagles and hawks, may build nests on mountain cliffs. Nests may be skillfully woven from twigs, weeds, mud, and other handy materials. A bird may even use pieces of old string, or bits of cloth or paper.

▲ **The emperor penguin does not eat anything for the two months that he incubates the egg. He must stay with it to make sure it does not touch the ice.**

▶ **Weaver birds make their nest from strands of grass or palms. The entrance to the nest faces down to deter enemies. There may be hundreds of nests in one tree.**

The strangest nest was probably one made by a sparrow in Switzerland. It was made entirely of watch springs.

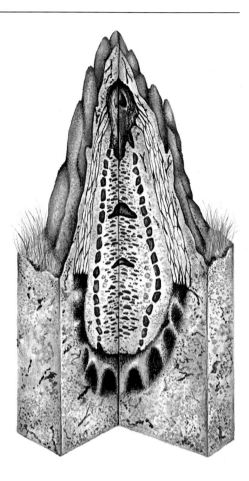

▲ **Above ground, the termite's nest is made of hard, mud walls that protect the cool, dark area below ground where the termites live.**

Some birds prefer to nest on the ground. But birds to not live in nests all year round. They usually build them as a place to lay eggs in, and as a home for the chicks after they hatch. Between mating seasons, birds sleep any place that provides shelter.

The homes of social insects (insects that live together in groups) are also called nests. You may have seen a paper wasps' nest hanging from a tree. It looks like a round, gray paper bag. In fact, the nest is really made of paper. The wasps gather bits of dead wood and other tough plants, and chew them into a papery pulp. This pulp is then used to form the nest. Inside, there are usually many *cells,* or rooms, in which the queen lays eggs and the grubs, or *larvae,* develop.

The nests of bees are called *hives.* They are often dome-shaped or round, and made of chewed plants and wax. Wax is produced by the bees' own bodies. Honeybees also use wax to make *honeycombs* inside the hive, with cells for storing honey and for hatching eggs.

Prairie dogs and hamsters are also skillful builders of underground homes. Their homes are called burrows. Each prairie dog builds its own home, close to the homes of other prairie dogs. Each scoops up a small mound at the entrance to its burrow. This serves as a sunning place and as a watching post.

Some large mammals, such as wolves, bears, and mountain lions, may not build their own homes. Instead, they find a cave to live in. Such cave homes are known as *dens* or *lairs.* The females give birth to

their young in the den. Bears use dens for their long winter sleep or *hibernation.* Certain kinds of bats live in caves, too.

Many other mammals have no home at all. Elephants, zebras, deer, and lions usually wander from place to place in groups or herds. Their needs are met by good feeding grounds, a water hole, and a temporary sleeping spot screened by trees or tall grass. But most animals, even if they do not build homes, occupy and defend a general area as their *territory.* An animal will stay within the limits of its territory as long as it has enough food there, and will try to keep other animals away. A red squirrel, for example, may consider certain trees its "private property." Any creature that tries to move into the trees will get a loud scolding.

▲ **Many spiders are expert web-spinners. This delicate trap of silk awaits flying insects. The spider pounces as soon as it senses prey struggling in the web.**

◄ **Harvest mice weave a ball-shaped nest of grasses. The nest hangs among the stalks of wheat.**

▶ ▶ ▶ ▶ **FIND OUT MORE** ◀ ◀ ◀ ◀
Animal Distribution; Ecology; Pet

LEARN BY DOING

Find out about different animal homes, and make drawings of them. What is a muskrat's home like? How is an eagle's nest different from the nest of a robin? If you keep pet animals, such as rabbits or hamsters, think about how these animals' man-made homes may differ from their wild relatives' homes. Look around your home and neighborhood, and you'll be surprised to see how many wild creatures are at home there, too.

ANIMAL INTELLIGENCE

SEE INTELLIGENCE

ANIMAL KINGDOM

A great many different kinds of animals live on earth. Scientists realized long ago that they needed some way to group, or classify, animals. They figured out a simple way to group the many different animals by the structures of their bodies.

It would take a long time and many details to describe completely a llama to someone who had never seen one. But if you said that the llama belongs to a family of long-necked, knobby-kneed mammals of the *artiodactyl* order, the person would already know, or could easily find out, a great deal about a llama.

Popular names for animals, such as "cat," "dog," or "llama" can describe very different animals in other countries of the world. So when a new animal is discovered, it is given a double personal scientific name by the discoverer. That name, the *genus* and *species* name, is recognized by scientists in every nation. Both genus and species are written in Latin. For example, the llama has the name *Lama glama*. No other animal has that same whole name. The vicuña, a relative of the llama, shares part of it. It is *Lama vicugna*. Both animals belong to the same genus, *Lama*.

A species is a group of animals so alike that they can mate and produce young that are, in their turn, able to reproduce. Animals of two different species but in the same genus usually cannot mate and reproduce. A llama and a vicuña would not naturally reproduce.

Relating the Species

A number of different *genera,* the plural of genus, make up a *family.* The llama belongs to the camel family. Three different genera make up

the camel family. Several different families make up an *order.* Llamas share the artiodactyl order with pigs, peccaries, hippopotamuses, deer, giraffes, and cattle among others. The members of all nine families in the order have three main things in common. First, they have an even number of toes on their feet. Second, their toes are covered with hoofs. Third, they have more than one chamber in their stomachs.

The order of even-toed hoofed animals shares a larger group, called a *class*, with many other orders. Carnivores, bats, elephants, rodents, and hoofed animals with an odd number of toes, make up some of the other orders in the class of animals called *mammals*. All mammals have body hair and feed their young with milk from the mothers' bodies. Most of them give birth to living young, but a few are so primitive that they lay eggs.

The animal kingdom is easily divided into animals with backbones called *vertebrates* and animals without backbones called *invertebrates*. Mammals, birds, fish, reptiles, and amphibians are all vertebrates. But all of these animals are only part of one of the big groups into which the animal kingdom is divided. Such a big group is called a *phylum*. All vertebrates and a few other creatures belong to the *chordate* phylum. Chordates have a special elastic rod inside the body that acts as an internal skeleton. In the vertebrates, that rod has hardened into a backbone.

There are so many different kinds of invertebrates (more than 950,000 known species) that scientists put them in 25 to 35 *phyla,* the plural of *phylum*. Not all scientists agree on the exact number of invertebrate phyla. Some animals do not fit tidily into the main phyla. For example, the animals called *velvet worms* are not quite *annelids* (segmented worms such as the earthworm) and not quite *arthropods* (animals with jointed legs and hard coverings like the crabs and

QUIZ

1. Which of these are not mammals: whales, humans, bats, alligators, kangaroos?
2. Can you name four members of the cat family?
3. Penguins come from eggs —but does the female or male penguin hatch them?
4. What do we call animals (such as most humans) that eat both meat and vegetables?

(Answers on page 256)

The giant tortoise lives longer than any other large animal. One lived for 177 years. But it is thought that some tiny bacteria can live many times as long.

insects). The velvet worms, although there are only about 80 species of them, are usually put into a small phylum of their own.

A Kingdom of Animal Phyla

A description of the animal kingdom by phyla usually starts out with the very simplest animals, whose bodies are single cells, and leads up to the complex chordates. This kind of an arrangement may be very closely related to the way in which animals probably evolved on earth.

The first single-celled animals were not very different from the first single-celled plants. But over millions of years, the differences between most plants and animals became greater. There are still some single-celled creatures that are not neatly "plant" or "animal." They are called *protists*, which means "simplest organisms." Most scientists classify protists in a kingdom of their own, apart from the animal and plant kingdoms.

The simplest animals are called *protozoans*, meaning "first animals." A protozoan consists of only a single cell, but that single cell takes in air, food, and water, and gets rid of wastes, all the basic work of living done by more complex animals. The largest protozoans are little more than one-eighth of an inch (3 mm) long. Most can be seen only through a microscope. Amoebas are microscopic protozoans that live in water.

All phyla except protozoa are made up of animals with many-celled bodies. They are called *metazoans*, which means "later animals." Some metazoans, such as sponges (phylum Porifera), are just masses of cells that are very much alike. More complicated animals than the sponge developed gradually over millions of years. Different groups of cells took on different tasks, and special systems of the body, such as the digestive system, developed. Animals that had heads and tails and shapes instead of just being blobs of living matter evolved, or developed.

The largest lobster is the American lobster. It can measure about 3 feet (1 m) in length and weigh up to 40 pounds (18 kg).

◄ Cats belong to the feline family and range in size from the lion and tiger to the small domestic cat (bottom left). The cat family also includes (left to right) the wild cat, lynx, black panther, and snow leopard.

The phylum Arthropoda includes centipedes, millipedes, and bristletails as well as the following classes (8,9,10):

8. Insecta. Examples of insects include butterflies, beetles, grasshoppers, bees, and ants.

9. Crustacea. Examples of crustaceans are crayfish, lobsters, and crabs.

10. Arachnida. Includes all spiders and scorpions.

7. Phylum Mollusca. Examples of mollusks include slugs, snails, clams, squids, and octopuses.

6. Phylum Annelida. Annelids include earthworms, leeches, and other worms with segmented bodies.

4. Phylum Platyhelminthes. Examples of platyhelminthes (flatworms) include flukes, tapeworms, and planaria.

3. Phylum Coelenterata. This group includes the sea anemones, corals, and jellyfish.

2. Phylum Porifera. All poriferans are sponges.

1. Phylum Protozoa. These are all microscopic, single-celled animals, such as amoebas.

16. Class Mammalia. Examples of mammals are kangaroos, rats and mice, moles, bats, seals, whales, cats, bears, horses, dogs, apes, elephants, and human beings.

13. Class Amphibia. Examples of amphibians are frogs, toads, and salamanders.

5. Phylum Nematoda. Also known as roundworms, the nematodes include many parasites.

11. Phylum Echinodermata. Examples of echinoderms are sea urchins and starfish.

15. Class Aves. This class includes all the birds—the only animals with feathers. Most of them can fly, but there are some flightless birds, such as the ostrich and the penguin.

14. Class Reptilia. Examples of reptiles are turtles, snakes, lizards, alligators, and crocodiles.

12. There are two main classes of fish: **Class Chondricthyes** (fish with skeletons of cartilage rather than bone, such as sharks and rays); and **Class Osteichthyes** (bony fish, such as goldfish and cod). Two other classes include: fish without jaws, such as the hagfish; and lungfish.

THE ANIMAL KINGDOM

INVERTEBRATES	
1. Protozoa	6. Annelids
2. Porifera	7. Mollusks
3. Coelenterates	8.–10. Arthropods
4. Flatworms	11. Echinoderms
5. Nematodes	**VERTEBRATES**
	12.–16. Chordates

So scientists group animals by the characteristics or features they have in common. Some of the characteristics cannot be easily seen by nonscientists. For example, there are many different kinds of wormlike animals. But they are put into several different phyla, depending on how complicated their digestive systems are, whether their bodies are smooth or segmented, and so on.

Future scientists studying fossils, evolution, genetics, and anatomy may find some answers to the mysteries of the animal kingdom.

▶▶▶▶ **FIND OUT MORE** ◀◀◀◀
Invertebrates see Amoeba; Centipedes and Millipedes; Coelenterate; Comb Jelly; Crustacean; Earthworm; Echinoderm; Insect; Mollusk; Protozoan; Spider; Sponge
Vertebrates see Amphibian; Bird; Fish; Mammal; Reptile
Science see Cell; Darwin, Charles; Evolution; Linnaeus, Carolus; Protist; Reproduction; Wallace, Alfred Russel

🔲 ANIMAL MOVEMENT

Many animals often move from one place to another. They search for food. They flee from danger. On land, animals walk, run, creep, leap, or glide. Many kinds of animals are also able to swim in water or fly through the air. Each kind of animal moves in the way that best helps it to survive.

Many land animals use legs and feet for speed. The cheetah, a wild cat of Africa, is called the fastest animal on Earth, but only for a short distance. A cheetah can *sprint* (run very quickly for a short distance) at up to 80 miles an hour (129 km/hr). Horses, deer, antelopes, and other speedy, hoofed animals have long, powerful legs. The longer an animal's legs are, the farther it can go in one step. The ostrich is the largest of all the birds. Its size means that it cannot fly but its legs are so strong that it can run faster than a horse. It is the fastest creature on two legs.

WHERE TO DISCOVER MORE

McGrath, Susan. *The Amazing Things Animals Do.* Washington, D.C.: National Geographic Society, 1989.

▼ **If this group of animals could have a level race against each other, the sailfish would just beat the cheetah, the fastest animal on land. The snail is the slowest creature in the race, though some insects are even slower. If a human being were in this race, he or she might be behind the giraffe but ahead of the elephant.**

mph | 1 | 80

LEARN BY DOING

Watch how different animals move. If you have a pet cat, notice how it walks, creeps, and runs. When a cat leaps down from a fence, which legs touch the ground first? Compare the way a cat walks with the way a dog walks. Watch horses and cows if you get the chance. Notice how these animals rise after lying down. What differences do you spot?

Make notes about the birds you see in your backyard or in the park. Do all birds run the same way on the ground? How about when they fly?

Watch how an earthworm moves. Does it move in the same way as a snake moves? If you visit a marine aquarium, look at fish and then at whales and dolphins. How do these animals use their tails when swimming?

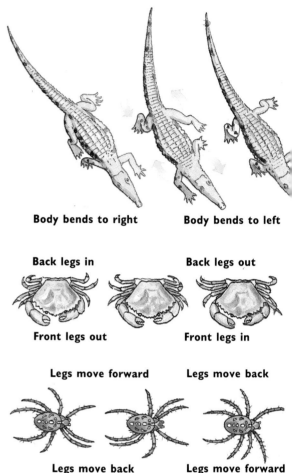

Body bends to right   **Body bends to left**

Back legs in   **Back legs out**

Front legs out   **Front legs in**

Legs move forward   **Legs move back**

Legs move back   **Legs move forward**

▶ **The crocodile bends its tail from left and right and arches its body from side to side as it moves along. A crab's limbs bend sideways under its body, making it move sideways instead of forward. A spider moves by taking its limbs forward, one after the other, and then back.**

▼ **Not until photography made possible stop-frame shots of running horses, in the 1800s, did people know for certain how a horse moved at speed.**

Insects have legs, too—six of them. Spiders have eight legs. Wormlike millipedes have up to 230 legs. Having so many legs can have many advantages, depending on the kind of animal. These three kinds of animals all have jointed legs. This is a great help in moving quickly, easily, and powerfully.

Some animals do not depend entirely on legs to go places in a hurry. Many monkeys and gibbons use their arms to swing through trees. Frogs can jump from danger in one sudden, long-distance hop.

Not all land animals have legs for walking and running. A snail uses one muscle, called a *foot*, to pull itself slowly along. A snake has muscles that move its body in an S-shaped curve, pushing against rough

spots on the ground. A fish can dart forward with a sideways flit of its tail fin. Like fish, whales and porpoises also use their tails for swimming power. But the tails of these sea mammals move up and down, rather than side to side. Squids and octopuses sometimes jet-propel from place to place. When one of these animals wants to move, it sucks in water and then shoots out a jet through a tube in its body. This stream of water pushes the animal in the opposite direction.

Most birds move about by flying. A bird's bones are light and hollow. They are light to allow the bird to fly more easily, but are strong enough to support the bird's body. Many adult insects, as well as bats (which are mammals) can also fly.

▶ ▶ ▶ ▶ **FIND OUT MORE** ◀ ◀ ◀ ◀
Animal; Bone; Flying Mammals;
Articles on individual animals

ANIMALS OF MYTH AND LEGEND

People told stories long ago of strange creatures and terrifying beasts. Some of the stories were myths, which often came from the religious beliefs of the people who told them. Other stories were legends, or popular stories that were handed down through the years. Legends and myths often told of animals that were not real. But people in earlier times believed they were. They did not know most of the scientific facts that people know today.

Some imaginary animals were part human. The *centaurs* of Greek mythology were half horse and half man. They were said to be wild and dangerous. They liked to fight and to destroy things. But one centaur, named Chiron, was kind and wise. Other Greek myths told of *satyrs,* gods of the woods. These mischievous creatures looked like men from the waist up, except for their pointed ears. From the waist down they looked like goats.

Mermaids were lovely creatures with a woman's body and a fish's tail. They were seen by sailors at sea, sitting on rocks and singing beautifully while combing their long golden hair. Some, called *sirens,* were very dangerous. Sailors passing by could not resist the sirens' singing. But when the sailors came near the island, their ships were wrecked on hidden rocks, and the sailors drowned.

The *unicorn* is perhaps the most beautiful of legendary animals. It appeared in both Greek and Roman mythology. This animal was pure white. It looked like a small horse, but it had a tail like a lion's, and on its forehead was a single horn. Even in the Middle Ages, people in Europe thought that the unicorn really existed.

Another fantastic animal was the *phoenix,* a bird with reddish purple feathers. Egyptian and Greek myths say that the phoenix lived to be 500 years old. The bird would then set fire to itself and burn to death. But from its ashes a new phoenix would arise. The phoenix became a symbol of *immortality* (life that lasts forever).

Monsters

Many stories tell of imaginary creatures that are evil and frightening. The *dragon* was a fire breathing serpent, or giant lizard. It appears in the myths and legends of many countries. In most stories, it was a horrible creature that often guarded a precious treasure. Only a brave hero could fight a dragon. In China, however, the dragon was regarded as a god, not an evil monster.

The *chimera* and the *basilisk* were monsters of Greek myth. The chimera had the head of a lion, the body of a goat, and the tail of a serpent. It breathed fire, like the dragon. People sometimes use the word "chimera" to mean a foolish or wild idea. The basilisk was a very nasty beast. It was a birdlike serpent that could kill people by breathing on them, or even just by looking at them.

In the Middle Ages people believed that the lizardlike salamander could pass through fire unharmed. Then, sometime later, a new material that could be spun and woven into fire-resistant fabric reached Europe. It was, people decided, salamander fur! Today we call it asbestos.

▲ Fierce griffins decorated palace walls in ancient Persia. The griffin was a royal guardian. It had a lion's body with eagle's wings.

▶ Greek legends told of Pegasus, the silver-winged horse of the gods. Here he carries his master Bellerophon, the young warrior who tamed him.

The Egyptians worshiped the cat. Killing a cat was a crime punishable by death. When a household cat died, its owner shaved off his eyebrows as a sign of grief.

▼ Dragons were sometimes good, sometimes evil. Here, Saint George, the patron saint of England, kills an evil dragon.

The *werewolf* was another unpleasant legendary monster. A werewolf was human by day, but at night turned into a wolf and killed people. The werewolf appeared in Greek myth, as well as in legends of other countries. Almost everyone has heard of *sea serpents*.

These monsters appear in legends all over the world, and in all ages. Such legends may have started when someone saw a real sea animal (such as a whale or giant squid) that was very strange and large. Some people claim that in Scotland today a giant serpentlike animal lurks in the depths of a great lake called Loch Ness. But scientists who have searched there have not yet located the monster.

Another legend still believed today is that of the abominable snowman or yeti. This is said to be a hairy, ape-like beast that lives in the Himalaya Mountains in Asia.

Animals with Special Powers

Not all legends tell of imaginary animals. Some tell of ordinary animals. But the legends show that people have thought that these ordinary animals had strange powers, or were special in some other way. The common house cat, for example, was worshiped as a god in ancient Egypt. The Hindus of India consider the cow a sacred animal. The Hindus will not allow cows to be killed, or even milked.

Animals play an important part in many Native American myths. In a story from California, the Creator tried twice to make Earth (which the Native Americans thought was flat) stable and safe. But Earth kept wobbling. So the Creator sent a deer, an elk, and a coyote to stand at the northern end of Earth in order to steady it. This didn't work either, because the animals floated in the air. Finally, the Creator made them lie down. From that time on, the myth says, Earth was usually still. But

Earth was disturbed by an earthquake if the animals moved. The Iroquois people, who lived in New York State, believed that Earth rested on the back of a very large turtle.

Babe, a giant blue ox, belonged to the legendary American giant lumberjack, Paul Bunyan. Babe was born white, but he turned blue in the Winter of the Blue Snow. He was so heavy that his feet sank down to solid rock at every step. The legend says that Babe's footprints formed the many lakes in Minnesota.

People have used the stories of fan-

tastic creatures to explain strange happenings that they could not explain in any other way. Or they may have created legends about animals to express their feelings about life.

▶ ▶ ▶ ▶ FIND OUT MORE ◀ ◀ ◀ ◀
Abominable Snowman; Bunyan, Paul; Fairy Tale; Folklore; Gods And Goddesses; Legend; Mythology

ANIMAL TRACKS

Animal tracks tell many stories. They are like written messages. They tell what kind of animal made them and in which direction it was going. They show whether it was hurrying, perhaps to escape an enemy, or taking its time. A person can learn to tell what an animal was doing by looking at its tracks.

A good time to track an animal—to follow its trail—is after a snowfall. A light snow, not deep enough for sledding, can be perfect for tracking an animal. Animal footprints may also be found in mud, dust, and sand. Even tracks left by wet or muddy feet on concrete pavement can be helpful in learning about tracking. At the beach, tracks of sandpipers and other shoreline birds are commonly seen near the water.

You can learn important clues, which help in tracking wild animals, from the footprints of dogs and cats. You will notice a large heel pad and four smaller toe pads if you look very carefully at the paw prints of a dog or cat. Cat tracks are rounder and smaller than the tracks of most dogs. Cat tracks almost never show claw marks, because cats usually keep their claws drawn back when walking or running. Dog footprints do show claw marks. These differences between footprints are the same among wild members of the dog families. Wolf and coyote tracks look like the footprints of large dogs. Tracks of wildcats, lynxes, and mountain lions look much like those of a house cat, except that they are larger and some will show claw marks.

The different ways in which animals move are also shown by their tracks. For example, rabbits hop. They put their long hind feet in front of their front feet with each bound. A set of rabbit tracks shows two prints of roundish forefeet just behind the longer marks of the hind feet. The trail sometimes zigzags with sets of

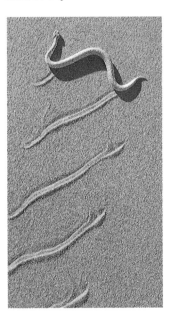

▼ As the sidewinder moves, only two points of the snake's body touch the hot desert sand at any one time.

◀ Greek legends tell of the Minotaur, a monster with the head of a bull and the body of a man. It lived in the Labyrinth (a mazelike building) on the island of Crete. The Minotaur was finally killed by Theseus, a Greek hero.

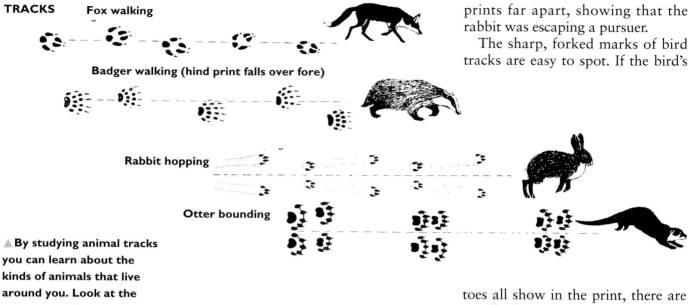

TRACKS

Fox walking

Badger walking (hind print falls over fore)

Rabbit hopping

Otter bounding

▲ **By studying animal tracks you can learn about the kinds of animals that live around you. Look at the tracks carefully to see how the animal might have been moving.**

prints far apart, showing that the rabbit was escaping a pursuer.

The sharp, forked marks of bird tracks are easy to spot. If the bird's toes all show in the print, there are usually three in front and one in back. The footprints of ducks and other swimming birds show the outlines of webbing between the toes.

Tracking is not always easy for a beginner. Few tracks are complete or perfect. Snow or dirt often falls on prints, covering or changing their shapes. The front feet of an animal may be different in size and shape from its back feet. But with practice and good detective work, animal tracking can become fascinating.

▶▶▶▶ **FIND OUT MORE** ◀◀◀◀
Animal Movement; Hands and Feet;
Nature Study

LEARN BY DOING

You can make copies, called *casts,* of animal tracks to collect and study. Find a clear print in the soil. Carefully remove loose leaves and twigs. Put a ring of heavy cardboard around the track. Into a bowl of water stir plaster of paris until it feels like a thick milkshake. Pour the plaster into the ring until the track is filled and the plaster touches the cardboard. Wait until the plaster is completely dry to remove the cast. You have made a *negative,* or upside-down, cast. You can also preserve the track as it was in the ground. To make such a *positive* cast, put a layer of petroleum jelly on the negative cast. Put it back in the cardboard ring, and pour plaster of paris onto the negative cast. When the plaster hardens, pull the two casts apart and wipe off the petroleum jelly.

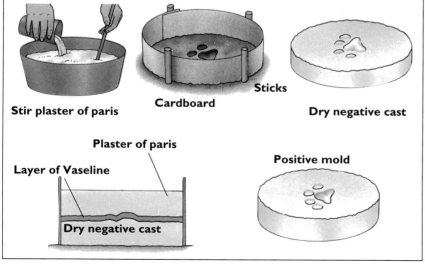

Stir plaster of paris

Cardboard

Sticks

Dry negative cast

Plaster of paris

Layer of Vaseline

Dry negative cast

Positive mold

ANIMAL VOICES

Many animals make sounds. Dogs bark, frogs croak, roosters crow, birds sing, lions roar. Animals use their voices to send messages. Sometimes the message is to one of their own kind: "Here I am, come and be friends." Sometimes the message is less friendly, and is meant as a warning: "Here I am, keep away."

One of the most important uses for an animal's voice is to help it find a mate. Mating calls may only be

<A killer whale. Like other cetaceans (whales and dolphins), it uses underwater sounds for communication with others of its species.

made at certain times of the year. In spring, male frogs croak to attract female frogs. Birds sing to attract mates and also to warn off rivals. The squawking blue jay may be telling

other birds, "Keep out of my tree!" Voices may be used to scare away enemies or to defend territory by warning others to stay outside. The loud roar of the male lion declares, "I'm the boss around here." Mother animals use their voices to call their young. For example, hens cluck to their chicks to keep them together.

Animals that live in groups, such as flocks or herds, often use voices to signal to each other. Flocks of wild geese honk. At sea, whales and porpoises swim in groups or schools and constantly give out whistles, grunts,

and other calls to one another. Animals that hunt in packs, such as wolves and coyotes, yelp and howl to signal others to join in the hunt. As a rule, herd animals are noisier than animals that spend most of their lives on their own.

Most animal voices are produced by *vocal cords* in the throat. When air passes from the lungs and across the cords, the cords vibrate and produce sounds. Animal vocal cords are in a "voice box." In mammals, the voice box is highly developed and is called a *larynx*. Birds have a simpler one, called a *syrinx*.

But not all animal sound signals are made by their vocal cords. Insects such as the cicada produce their high-pitched mating calls by rubbing together parts of their bodies or by vibrating membranes on their bodies. Insects do not have proper voices, but can make a variety of buzzing and chirping noises in this way.

▶ ▶ ▶ ▶ **FIND OUT MORE** ◀ ◀ ◀ ◀
Singing; Sound; Speech

The noise blue whales make when they are "talking" to each other has been measured at up to 188 decibels, making it the loudest sound emitted by any living creature. The whale voices have been detected up to 350 miles (850 km) away.

◀ **Grasshoppers make sounds by rubbing two parts of their body together. Courting males make the loudest noises.**

ANNAPOLIS

SEE U.S. SERVICE ACADEMIES

▲ **Spectacular fireworks displays are used to celebrate special anniversaries such as Independence Day.**

ANNIVERSARY

An anniversary is a day celebrated each year in memory of a special event. Your birthday is the anniversary of the day on which you were born. In many places in the United States, people also celebrate the birthday of a famous person whom they admire, such as Abraham Lincoln on February 12, and Martin Luther King Jr. on January 15.

Another kind of anniversary celebrates the "birth" of a state or a nation. Many U.S. states have celebrated their centennial—the 100th anniversary of the date on which they became states. One of the most popular national holidays in the United States is the Fourth of July, the anniversary of the country's birth as an independent nation. The United States celebrated its bicentennial—its 200th "birthday"—on July 4, 1976. This anniversary was so important, it was celebrated the whole year long.

Another common anniversary is the wedding anniversary, which marks the date when a couple was married. The three major wedding anniversaries, named for the type of gift that is often given, are the *silver* after 25 years of marriage, the *golden* after 50 years, and the *diamond* anniversary after 60 years.

▶▶▶▶ **FIND OUT MORE** ◀◀◀◀
Holiday

ANT

The insects called ants live almost everywhere, from jungles to cities to mountains to deserts. Ants are "colonial" insects. They live in citylike *colonies,* made up of large numbers of insects that work together and help each other to survive. They fight wars with other colonies. You can usually spot an opening to an underground colony by the little mound of soil around it—the anthill. Other kinds of ants live in dead trees or even in houses.

There are several thousand different kinds of ants. All of them belong to the same order of insects as bees and wasps. All of these insects have *constricted* (pinched-in) abdomens and, when winged, have four clear, many-veined wings in two pairs, one smaller than the other.

The bodies of adult ants have three main parts: head, thorax, and abdomen. On the front of the head are two *antennae* (feelers). Ants use

An ant can lift 50 times its own weight. This is about equal to your lifting a weight of two tons (4,000 lb).

▶ **Weaver ants make their nests by fastening together the edges of leaves with sticky strands produced by grubs.**

these for smelling, tasting, and touching. The thorax is the middle section of the body. The insect's six legs are attached to the thorax. Most kinds of male ants and most young queens have wings for a while, and these are attached to the thorax, too. The stomach and intestines are in the abdomen of the ant.

In each ant colony, there is usually just one *queen,* a small number of *males,* and a great many *workers.* Queens are usually larger than the other ants in the colony. They may live 20 years, and a single queen may lay millions of eggs. Male ants live only a few weeks. They die after they mate with a queen. Nearly all the ants in a colony are females called workers. The workers do not lay eggs. Instead they have several important jobs. Some take care of the queen. Others are "nurses," who care for the young. Others *forage* (hunt) for food for the whole colony. And still others are soldiers and guards.

The queens and males usually fly from the nest to mate. The males then die. But the queens are ready to begin new colonies. After mating, a queen lays many eggs. Some eggs are fertilized and will become females. Others are not and will become males. The eggs hatch after several days or weeks into white, wormlike *larvae* or grubs. "Nurse" ants feed and clean the larvae, and carry them if they must be moved. A few female larvae are fed special food. They will develop into new queens. The larvae become *pupas* after a few weeks or months.

Pupas appear to be inactive, or resting. The pupas of some kinds of ants are covered by a silklike cocoon. Many internal changes are going on during the pupa stage. These changes take place even though pupas cannot move about and do not have to be fed. Pupas finally emerge as full-sized adult ants.

The Ways Ants Live

Different kinds of ants lead very different lives.

Leaf-cutters have jaws with sharp edges. The workers bite off pieces of leaves and flowers. They carry the pieces to their nest, where they make large piles. The queen plants bits of mushroom in these piles, and the mushroom "garden" that grows up provides food for the colony.

Harvester ants gather and store seeds in their nests. They thus always have a supply of food. The ants crush the seeds with their heavy jaws and make a soft pulp called *ant bread.* If the seeds get wet, the harvesters carry them outside to dry and

There are more ants than any other social insect. At any time there are at least a quadrillion living ants on earth (1,000,000,000,000,000).

▼ Inside an ants' nest, each ant has its own special job as part of the colony. Some collect food, others look after the young. There are builders, cleaners, and soldiers. The most important ant in the nest is the queen.

Worker ants with larvae

Adult ant emerging from pupa

Queen ant laying eggs

Worker ants with aphids

Wood ant

▶ **Four kinds of ants found in North America. Some ants are serious pests, such as the fire ant of the South, which feeds on seeds and has a painful sting.**

bring the seeds back into the nest at night.

Certain insects, such as *aphids,* are plant suckers. These insects produce a sticky, sweet fluid called *honeydew,* which some ants eat. The *cow-keeping ants* use aphids as cows. They may "milk" the aphids for the honeydew by stroking them, or actually eat the insects. The ants do not, however, really "herd" or tend the aphids although the ants will protect the aphids from various enemies by using their jaws and stingers.

Honey ants eat honeydew, too. But instead of milking aphids, they gather their supply from the leaves where plant-sucking insects drop their honeydew. Sometimes worker honey ants store the honey in their bodies. They often get so big and fat that they cannot move. Other ants in the colony get their honey from the mouths of these "living bottles."

Other ants, called *amazons,* are ferocious warriors. Their sharp, curved jaws are good for fighting but not for working. These ants keep slaves. They kidnap pupas from other nests. When the pupas develop, the captives spend all their adult lives

Red ant

Honey ant

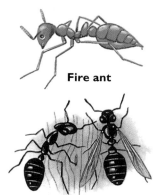

Fire ant

Carpenter ant

working for the amazons.

Some other ferocious ants are the African *drivers* and their close relatives, the South American *army ants.* These ants do not build nests. They rest under logs or rocks for two or three weeks, while larvae are being hatched. Then the whole colony "marches" about looking for food. These ants will eat other insects, young birds, and even small mammals that cannot get out of the way of their marching column. Most army ant colonies have between 10,000 and several million members.

Friend or Foe?

Ants are a help to people most of the time. Ants, like earthworms, turn the soil and let air mix with it. Also ants pollinate some plants. Many ants eat other insects, some of which are harmful pests. By chewing up scraps of plant and animal stuff in their tunnels, ants and their grubs help enrich soil.

Ants do not always help people, however. Leaf-cutters ruin many plants. *Fire ants* have become a serious pest in the southern United States. They have a bite that can kill small animals and make people ill. They also build large mounds in fields that interfere with farm machinery. Some ants are household pests. *Carpenter ants,* for example, can damage buildings by making tunnels in wooden beams. But overall, the damage that ants can do is not so important as the help that they give people.

▶▶▶▶ **FIND OUT MORE** ◀◀◀◀
Anteater; Insect; Metamorphosis; Terrarium

LEARN BY DOING

Watch what happens when you disturb an ants' nest. See how the workers carry the eggs and larvae to safety. You can study the fascinating world of ants at leisure by carefully pushing a sheet of clear glass through the middle of the nest. Clear away the loose earth from the front of the glass, so that you can see into the nest. Behind the glass wall, the ants will go about their lives undisturbed. What happens when the new queens are ready to leave the nest?

ANTARCTICA

The southern continent of Antarctica is a great sheet of snow and ice. The snow and ice slope gently toward the sea from a central *plateau,* a high, level area, around the South Pole. Along the coasts of Antarctica, sharp mountains rise up from the snow. Huge masses of ice called *glaciers* slide between the mountain ridges and down toward the sea. At the sea's edge, enormous icebergs break off and float away. One iceberg is said to have been the size of Delaware.

The Land and Snow

Beneath the snow and ice of Antarctica lies land. Snow piles deeper and deeper on top of the land and hardens into ice. In some places, it is 3 miles (4.8 km) deep. Near this great frozen land mass is a chain of smaller islands. One of the islands has an active volcano, Mount Erebus. The islands and the land mass are joined by a thick blanket of ice.

Antarctica has nine-tenths of all the world's ice. If all this ice melted, the level of the world's oceans would rise 250 feet (76 m). Most cities along the coast would be drowned. In New York harbor, water would almost cover the Statue of Liberty. But Antarctica stays well below freezing all year in most places. It is the coldest place on Earth. Inland, winter temperature falls to −100°F (−73°C).

Antarctica is actually a desert. Most people think of a desert as a very hot and dry place. Antarctica is certainly not hot, but it is very dry. All its water is frozen. Only about 5 inches (130 mm) of snow fall each year, which is less moisture than some of the world's hot, sandy deserts receive each year. The little snow that does fall on Antarctica piles up over the years, because not much of it melts.

Plant and Animal Life

Like other deserts, Antarctica does not have much plant life. Only a few kinds of trees and simple plants, such as mosses, lichens, and algae, can grow there. The climate is so harsh and food so scarce, that people have not settled in Antarctica. But along the coasts of the continent there are many birds, fish, and mammals.

The Antarctic waters are rich in *plankton,* tiny sea creatures and plants that provide food for fish and whales. Many seals and whales swim in Antarctic seas. Six kinds of seals are found. The fur seal, the smallest, has long been hunted for its silky fur. The leopard seal, which can grow up to 12 feet (3.6 m) long, has powerful jaws and sharp teeth. It eats fish and penguins. The elephant seal, the largest, can weigh as much as 4 tons (3.6 metric tons). Other kinds of seals are the Ross, Weddell, and crabeater.

The blue whale is the largest animal on Earth. It may weigh as much

ANTARCTICA

Area
About 5,500,000 square miles (14,244,000 sq. km)

Coastline
About 13,800 miles (22,208 km) long

Highest point
Mount Vinson Massif, 16,864 feet (5,140 m)

Lowest point
Sea level

Population
No permanent residents. Many scientists and explorers visit the continent to study the area.

Resources
Large coal deposits in east Antarctica. Probably other minerals. Fish and plankton in the surrounding seas.

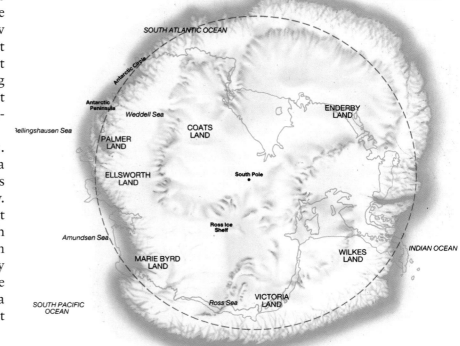

▲ Antarctica is covered by ice, but peaks called munataks stick up in places at the coast. The ice breaks off to form huge flat-topped icebergs.

Antarctic fish do not freeze solid when the sea freezes. This is because their blood contains a natural "antifreeze"— a complex chemical substance that stops the formation of ice crystals in the fishes' bodies.

▼ Antarctica's wildlife must be hardy to survive. Penguins have a thick layer of fat around their bodies. Seals also have a layer of fat, as well as short, dense fur that forms a water-proof coat.

as 150 tons (136 metric tons) and be 95 feet (30 m) long. Smaller whales include the bottlenose, the humpback, the sperm, and the finback.

A number of birds live in Antarctica. Petrels, terns, cape pigeons, and skuas fly over the water and ice. The Arctic tern has been called the long-distance champion flier. Each year it migrates between the northernmost islands of the Arctic (the region around the North Pole) and the shores of Antarctica, a distance of about 11,000 miles (17,700 km).

Penguins are the best known of Antarctic birds. They cannot fly, but their flipperlike wings make them strong swimmers. Penguins eat fish. The large emperor penguin looks as if it were dressed in a tuxedo for a formal dinner. The Adélie penguin, which is smaller than the emperor, lives in large colonies along the coast and seems to enjoy getting in the way of scientists working in Antarctica.

Exploring the Icy Continent

Antarctica was the last continent to be discovered. Explorers had long wondered if a southern polar continent existed. In 1772, Captain James Cook, a British explorer, started a three-year voyage in which he sailed completely around Antarctica but never saw the mainland.

In 1820, Americans hunting for fur seals were the first to sight the "forgotten continent." But Antarctica was not proved to be a continent until 1840, when the American naval lieutenant Charles Wilkes completed a voyage along the coast.

The "race to the South Pole" between a Norwegian explorer, Roald Amundsen, and a British explorer, Robert F. Scott, took place in 1911. Amundsen and his men reached the Pole first and returned safely. Scott and his men got there a month later. But they died from cold and lack of supplies on the return trip.

A later explorer, Sir Hubert Wilkins of Australia, was the first to fly over Antarctica in 1928. Admiral Richard E. Byrd of the U.S. Navy flew over the South Pole in 1929. (Byrd was also the first man to fly over the North Pole.) In 1929, Byrd set up a permanent base camp called *Little America* on the Ross Ice Shelf.

Sir Vivian Fuchs led a British Commonwealth expedition that was the first to cross Antarctica from coast to coast in 1958.

An agreement made in 1959 and now signed by 32 nations says that none will claim territory for itself in Antarctica or use it for military purposes. In 1991, a 50 year ban on mining was added to the treaty.

People are worried, however, about the pollution that drifts to the Antarctic from other parts of the world. In 1984, scientists discovered a hole in the ozone layer over the Antarctic, caused by air pollution.

There is now a permanent manned base at the South Pole. Scientists go to Antarctica to measure glaciers, study weather, and learn more about its history and rocks, its plants and animals. Antarctica has been called "the world's greatest scientific laboratory."

▶ ▶ ▶ ▶ **FIND OUT MORE** ◀ ◀ ◀ ◀
Aerosol; Amundsen, Roald; Arctic; Byrd, Richard E.; Continent; Cook, Captain James; Earth; Exploration; Glacier; Penguin; Scott, Robert F.; Seals and Sea Lions; Whales and Whaling

ANTEATER

Several different animals are called anteaters because they eat mainly ants or termites ("white ants"). Many anteaters have heads and mouths adapted for gathering their food. For example, the aardvark, sometimes called the *cape anteater,* has a narrow head and a sticky tongue. The echidna or *spiny anteater* of Australia does, too. The pangolins of Africa and Asia, which look like armadillos, are also known as *scaly anteaters.* They look like insect-eating pinecones, especially when they curl up inside their shields of overlapping scales.

Mainly, however, the name *anteater* is used for three mammals that

MAJOR EVENTS IN ANTARCTICA	
1772	Captain James Cook sailed around Antarctica, but sighted no land.
1838–40	Lieutenant Charles Wilkes proved Antarctica was a continent by sailing along its coast.
1911	Roald Amundsen first reached the South Pole, beating Robert F. Scott.
1928	Sir Hubert Wilkins became the first man to fly over Antarctica.
1929	Admiral Richard E. Byrd sets up a permanent base camp in Antarctica called Little America on the Ross Ice Shelf.
1947	Admiral Richard E. Byrd led Operation Highjump, the largest Antarctica expedition ever organized up to that time.
1956	The United States Navy started to establish permanent bases.
1957–58	Scientists participating in the International Geophysical Year studied all aspects of Antarctica.
1967	Peter J. Barrett found fossils proving that Antarctica once had a warmer climate.
1984	Scientists discovered a huge hole in the ozone layer over Antarctica.
1985	Twenty-four nations met in Antarctica itself to discuss the Antarctic Treaty, and how best to use Antarctica for the world's benefit.

live in the hot, humid forests of Central and South America. Like armadillos and sloths, these mammals lack some or all of the usual mammal teeth. The order of mammals to which armadillos, sloths, and anteaters belong is called *Edentata,* which means "toothless." Anteaters have no teeth at all. They have a tubelike mouth containing a long tongue. They have strong, curved claws for breaking open termite nests.

Female anteaters usually give birth to only one baby a year. It rides on the mother's back for several weeks after it is born.

The largest of the three American anteaters is the *giant anteater.* It lives on the ground. Its body is about three feet (90 cm) long, with a bushy tail that adds another three feet. It has a gray-brown coat. On its shoulders are black marks edged in white. The body color blends with sunlight and shadow, helping to hide the animal from its enemies. The giant anteater wanders alone, searching for food, stopping only to curl up and sleep. It is sometimes called an antbear.

The *tamandua,* or *collared anteater,* is only half as big as the giant anteater. The tamandua lives in

▲ **A mother tamandua, or collared anteater, with her baby clinging to her back. She is feeding on a termite nest in a tree. Her tongue can reach up to 10 inches.**

▼ The giant anteater's front claws are so long that the animal has to walk on the sides of its feet.

trees, where it can cling to branches with its strong, almost hairless tail. Its fur is yellow-brown with a darker vest and collar.

The smallest anteater is the *dwarf anteater*, also called the *silky* or *two-toed anteater*. It is about the size of a large squirrel. Unlike the stiff fur of other anteaters, its golden hair is very soft and silky. The animal often lives in silk-cotton trees, which bear silk-like fruit pods that match the anteater's fur coat. The silky anteater can grip the tree with its tail.

▶▶▶▶ **FIND OUT MORE** ◀◀◀◀
Aardvark; Armadillo; Mammal;
Sloth; Spiny Anteater

ANTELOPE

Antelopes are grazing animals known for their speed, their graceful high leaps, and their beautiful, curiously shaped horns. Their closest relatives are cattle. Both antelopes and cattle are *ungulates* (hoofed animals). Antelopes, like cattle, have an even number of hoofed toes, and horns instead of antlers. They eat plants, and they chew cuds.

Antelopes are fast-moving, nervous animals. They need to be alert, for they are a favorite prey of meat-eating animals such as lions. Antelopes must be prepared to eat their food and run. Later, in safety, the animals chew *cuds* (balls) of the plant food they swallowed earlier.

Animals that chew cuds are called *ruminants*.

Deer are ruminants, too. But deer have antlers made of bone that are shed and replaced every year. Antelopes have horns that grow only once in a lifetime. Both male and female antelopes usually have horns.

There are almost 100 kinds of antelopes, differing mainly in size and kinds of horns. The tiny *royal antelope*, which looks like a rodent, lives in forested western Africa. Its small horns barely show above the hair on its head. The *sable* is a large horselike antelope of southern and eastern Africa. Its magnificent horns can be up to 4 feet (1.2 m) long and curve backward in an arc. The desert-living *common oryx* has short, perfectly straight horns. The *blackbuck* of India has ringed horns that look like giant corkscrews. The *impala* of the African savanna or grassy plains, has horns shaped like a lyre, a small musical instrument similar to a harp.

Antelopes also differ in their living conditions. Many kinds live in deserts, far from water. The *addax* lives in the Sahara Desert of northern Africa. It

The word "antelope" comes from the Greek *antholopos,* meaning brightness-of-eye. Antelopes' eyes are very large and bulging. This allows the animals to look around without moving their heads.

▶ The waterbuck is native to the area of Africa south of the Sahara Desert. It lives by wet marshland rather than the drier grassland that many antelopes prefer.

has large hoofs that keep it from sinking in sand. The little water it gets comes from plant roots, which it digs out of the sand.

The graceful *gazelles* live on open plains in Africa and Asia. They are small- to medium-sized animals with lyre-shaped horns. A *springbok* gazelle can leap 10 feet high (3 m) or cover 20 feet (6 m) in one jump while running at a speed of 65 miles an hour (105 km/hr).

The large and very heavy *giant eland* of forests and plains in western Africa looks more like an ox than an antelope. The *brindled* gnu or *wildebeest* is also like an ox, but it gallops quickly when pursued by lions.

The *duiker* lives in thick underbrush in African forests. It is no bigger than a large rabbit. The *reedbuck* lives in marshes, where it wades for plants to eat.

The *pronghorn,* an animal that North Americans call an "antelope," actually belongs in a different family from real antelopes. It has horns that are shed every year. The male's horns are 12 inches (30 cm) long and have small prongs curving toward the front near the top.

The pronghorn is America's fastest mammal and also one of its rarest. When a pronghorn in the herd sees danger, it raises the white patch of hair on its rump as a warning signal to the others. Pronghorns can run 60

miles an hour (97 km/hr) for a short time. Coyotes hunt pronghorns by taking turns to chase them, until the pronghorns are exhausted.

▶ ▶ ▶ ▶ FIND OUT MORE ◀ ◀ ◀ ◀
Deer; Hoofed Animals; Horns and Antlers; Mammal

☼ ANTENNA

Look closely the next time you see a butterfly or bumblebee. You will notice two long, narrow "feelers" extending from its head. Each of these feelers is called an *antenna.*

Antennae (the plural of antenna) usually occur in pairs—crustaceans such as lobsters and crabs have two pairs. Antennae are used by insects, snails, and some types of shellfish to receive signals of taste, touch, or smell. Some shellfish even use their antennae to help them swim. Others use them as anchors, in order to

attach themselves to rocks. A male mosquito's antennae have hairs that are sensitive to sound. They can hear the sound of female mosquitoes up to a quarter of a mile (0.4 km) away.

A radio or television also uses an antenna to receive signals. This type of antenna is spelled "antennas" in the plural. Televisions and radios are sometimes called *receivers,* because they receive *radio waves.* These messages start out as electrical signals at the television or radio station. A *transmitter* at the station converts these signals to radio waves that are sent out from a transmitting antenna.

▲ The antennae of a cockroach pick up movements in the air around them, warning the insect of approaching danger. It can then run and hide.

> The largest antelope is the Eland. It is about 6 feet (1.8 m) high at the shoulder and weighs about a ton. Its spiral horns grow to a length of 4 feet (1.2 m).

Your radio or television picks up these waves with its antenna, which then converts them back to electrical signals. The electrical signals are turned into sounds you can hear or pictures you can see.

An antenna shaped like a dish acts like a mirror. It picks up weak signals and reflects them back to a small antenna, called the *focus,* at the center of the dish. A television with a *dish antenna* can pick up special signals that are reflected off *satellites.*

Astronomers also use dish antennas, or *radio telescopes,* to pick up radio signals from distant stars. The Arecibo Observatory in Puerto Rico has one of the world's largest radio telescopes. It stretches 1,000 feet (305 m) across a natural valley.

ANTHONY, SUSAN B.

SEE WOMEN'S RIGHTS

who try to solve these secrets are called *anthropologists.*

Anthropo is the ancient Greek word for human being. So "anthropology" means the science of human beings. It is a fairly recent science, which began in the 19th century.

Most anthropologists concentrate on one of the four main branches of anthropology: physical anthropology, archeology, cultural anthropology, and linguistics. The *physical anthropologist* wants to know how and when people began to do things that no other animal can do. Physical anthropologists often study ancient human bones that have been found deep in the ground. By comparing these bones with the bones of modern humans, they can learn how the human body has changed over hundreds of thousands of years. Physical

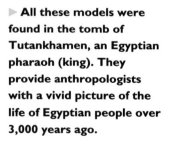

▶ **All these models were found in the tomb of Tutankhamen, an Egyptian pharaoh (king). They provide anthropologists with a vivid picture of the life of Egyptian people over 3,000 years ago.**

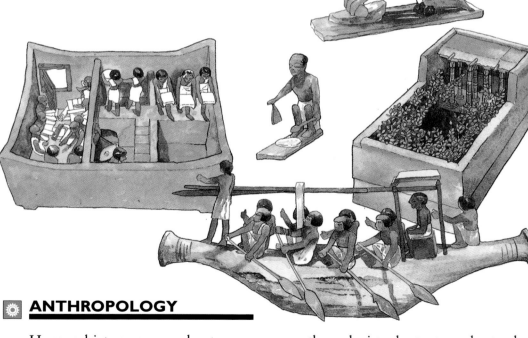

☼ ANTHROPOLOGY

Human history seems short compared to that of rocks, oceans, fish, other mammals, birds, and other features of the Earth.

But there are still many puzzles about human beings and how they developed the way they did. People

anthropologists also try to understand why there are different groups of humans—why, for example, do some people have brown skin, while others have white or yellow skin? They compare the groups to see how they are alike as well as how they are different.

The *archeologist* is interested in learning how the people of ancient civilizations lived. What did they wear? What kind of food did they eat? What did they believe? What were their customs? Archeologists dig in the earth, looking for tools, clothing, or pottery that might give a clue about the lives of the people who once used them. One of the most important archeological discoveries has been the Valley of the Kings, near Cairo, Egypt. This place was a cemetery for the *pharaohs* (kings) of Egypt more than 3,000 years ago. From the more than 60 tombs discovered so far, archeologists have found out many things about how the ancient Egyptians lived and what they thought.

The *cultural anthropologist* is concerned with the everyday life of people living today. These scientists study the customs, arts, beliefs, governments, and economy of a people. A cultural anthropologist can also be called an *ethnologist,* which means "one who studies people."

Ethnology in the past was the study of people in isolated areas of the world, far from civilization. Ethnologists offered explanations for cultures, languages, and races in terms of historical migrations. They

▲ Anthropologists often study funeral and burial customs of ancient peoples. This tall stone is a menhir, a funeral monument built in the Bronze Age.

found it easier to study small groups, such as the aborigines of Australia, who still lived much like their ancestors did thousands of years ago.

Today, ethnologists or cultural anthropologists are comparing past and present cultures to learn how racial and ethnic groups have changed. They are particularly interested in how people from ancient cultures adapt to modern life, with its complex machines and scientific inventions. To study these groups,

▼ Anthropologists study the way that human beings have developed. They have found skulls and bones of apelike people who lived over two million years ago, called Australopithecus. Over time, human beings stood straighter and taller. The skull began to change shape as the brain grew larger.

Australopithecus

Homo habilis

Homo erectus

Neanderthal man

Modern man

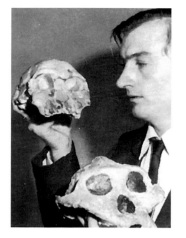

▲ **Richard Leakey, the anthropologist, compares the cast of a skull 22 million years old (top) with that of a million-year-old Australopithecus.**

▶ **A mold of** *penicillium.* **Fleming, Florey, and Chain helped turn this natural growth into an antibiotic that saved thousands of lives.**

The use of molds as antibiotics is not a recent discovery. The Chinese, 2,500 years ago, used the molding curd of soybeans to treat boils and other infections.

anthropologists may live with them for a while.

Some anthropologists make a special study of *linguistics*, the science of language. By studying the language of a people, the linguist can learn much about their knowledge and beliefs. Many linguists are particularly interested in languages that are spoken but have never been written down, such as those of certain Native American and African tribes. Other linguists study "dead" languages—those that are no longer spoken, such as Old Hebrew, or written, such as ancient Egyptian hieroglyphics.

Applied anthropology uses what anthropologists have discovered to help solve modern problems. Anthropology can shed new light on how our bodies grow, what foods are good for us, and why some people commit crimes.

Anthropologists have done much to help people of different cultures understand one another. One of the most famous American anthropologists was Margaret Mead (1901–1978).

▶▶▶▶ **FIND OUT MORE** ◀◀◀◀
Aborigine; Archeology; Culture; Customs; Human Being; Sociology

ANTIBIOTIC

Antibiotics are substances that help the body fight against bacteria and other germs. Doctors use antibiotics to treat diseases caused by bacteria. When someone is sick with such a disease, a series of shots or pills of an antibiotic can cure or control the disease. Millions of lives have been saved since antibiotics were first used in 1941. Most antibiotics are produced naturally by plants so small they can be seen only under a microscope. Most antibiotics that doctors

use are produced by *molds*. Molds are a type of *fungus*, a simple plant that cannot make its own food.

Today, many different antibiotics are used to treat infections. Penicillin, the first antibiotic used in medicine, is still the best known. It was discovered accidentally in 1928 by

Alexander Fleming, a British scientist. He noticed that a certain blue-green mold stopped the growth of bacteria. He tried unsuccessfully for more than ten years to separate from the mold the chemicals that stopped bacterial growth. He finally succeeded in 1940, with the aid of two other scientists, Howard Florey and Ernst Chain. They named the new drug "penicillin" after *Penicillium notatum*, the mold that produces it.

The first person treated with penicillin was a policeman dying of blood poisoning. Florey injected penicillin into the man's veins, and he began to get better. But there was not enough penicillin in the shot to stop completely the growth of the bacteria poisoning his blood. He became ill again, but Florey had no more penicillin. So the policeman died.

Although the patient died, Florey had proved that bacterial infections could be successfully treated with penicillin. All Florey needed was a large quantity of penicillin. He went to the United States and there persuaded drug companies to grow *penicillium* mold. The companies produced large amounts of penicillin during World War II and saved thousands of lives.

Scientists have found many more useful antibiotics, such as the sulfa drugs, and *Aureomycin*, *Chloromycetin*, and *Terramycin*, all of which are effective against different bacterial diseases.

Scientists have become worried because many disease-causing bacteria are becoming resistant to the effects of some antibiotics. As a result, many doctors want to limit how often antibiotics are used.

▶▶▶▶ **FIND OUT MORE** ◀◀◀◀
Bacteria; Disease; Drug; Drug Abuse; Fleming, Sir Alexander; Fungus; Medicine

ANTIDOTE

SEE FIRST AID; POISON

ANTIGEN AND ANTIBODY

If an army breaks into a fort, the soldiers inside fight to push the enemy out. The body defends itself against disease in a similar way. *Antigens* are parts of foreign invaders: any disease-causing agents, such as bacteria, snake poisons, or viruses, or even harmless substances like pollen. The body makes weapons, or *antibodies*, to fight the invading antigens.

A human body makes large amounts of antibody when an infection strikes. Antibodies are made in special places, such as in the glands under the arm or in the tonsils in the throat. These glands become large and active when they must produce great amounts of antibodies. So people get swollen throats and necks or

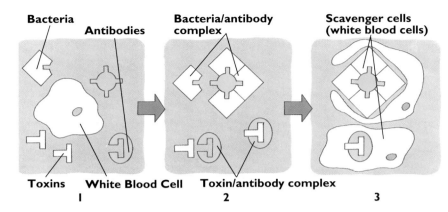

Bacteria — Antibodies — Bacteria/antibody complex — Scavenger cells (white blood cells)

Toxins — White Blood Cell — Toxin/antibody complex

1   2   3

lumps in the armpits when they are sick with certain diseases.

Antibodies travel through the bloodstream to the infected parts of the body. They are chemical agents that prevent the growth and spread of bacteria or viruses. Often, in a few days, the antibodies overcome the virus, and the person feels better. Sometimes, though, the sick person will need medicine to help, too.

If a person is "attacked" by the measles virus, the antibodies "remember," and if the virus attacks the body again, the antibodies can often remove the invader so quickly that the person will not even feel ill. If a person has had measles, he or she will probably not get it again—they have *immunity* to it. The body becomes immune to most common diseases. Vaccination can also produce immunity.

▶▶▶▶ **FIND OUT MORE** ◀◀◀◀
Blood; Disease; Immunity

ANTIGUA AND BARBUDA

SEE WEST INDIES

ANTILLES

SEE WEST INDIES

▲ The steps taken by white blood cells to defend the body against infection: 1. Bacteria invade the blood and produce toxins. In defense, white blood cells produce antibodies. 2. The antibodies attack the bacteria and toxins (antigens) and lock on to them. 3. White blood cells then engulf the antigens and digest them.

▲ Vaccinations are given to children to protect them from diseases. The vaccine is made up of weakened antigens injected into the body, causing protective antibodies to be produced. Sometimes further vaccinations, or boosters, are needed to provide continuing protection.

Some people think that there may be some galaxies far away from us in the universe that are made entirely of antimatter.

ANTIMATTER

Scientists keep finding more and more tiny particles inside the atom. They have also found out that all these particles have twin particles that are exactly the same as their corresponding ordinary particles except that they have the opposite electrical charge. These particles are called *antiparticles* and they make up *antimatter.*

The antiparticles to the electrons that spin around the center of atoms are called *positrons.* Electrons have a negative electrical charge; positrons have an exactly equal and opposite positive charge.

Antimatter does not exist naturally on Earth. If it did it would meet ordinary matter and there would be a tremendous explosion. Whenever an antiparticle meets an ordinary particle the two destroy each other and there is a burst of radiation. However, scientists can produce short-lived antiparticles in *particle accelerators.*

▶ ▶ ▶ ▶ **FIND OUT MORE** ◀ ◀ ◀ ◀
Atom; Matter

ANTIQUE

The skillful artists of the ancient world created beautiful objects, such as sculpture and jewelry. Sculptors often worked with materials that they knew would last, such as bronze, marble, or other stones. Jewelers worked with gold, silver, and precious gems. Many such works of art were collected by people who valued beautiful objects. Greece and Rome produced many valuable works of art. Long after Greece and Rome were no longer great powers in the world, some of these treasures were preserved.

During the Renaissance period in Europe (which lasted from the 1400s to the 1600s), wealthy people started to collect objects from the ancient world. They called these objects *antiques.* Antiques were valued because they were a record of the past, as well as being beautiful old objects.

The word "antique" slowly grew in meaning to include any very old object that is valued as a work of art or that reminds people of an earlier time. Antiques are often costly works of art such as paintings or sculpture, but they can also be practical items such as furniture, lamps, household utensils, tools, musical instruments, and fine carpets. Traditionally, antiques have been grouped into four main categories: furniture, ceramics (china), glass, and metal.

Some collectors think that an object must be at least 100 years old to be an antique, and this is the standard used by the United States government. But people collect newer objects that have a nostalgic or rarity

▲ Many people collect Greek and Roman antiques. Here is a Greek vase called an amphora. The Greeks painted scenes on their vases, showing heroes and gods.

▼ Antique toys such as teddy bears and model cars have become very valuable. The teddy bear was introduced in the early 1900s and named after President Theodore Roosevelt. Early teddy bears were handmade, while other toys, such as the model car, were often made in factories.

value, such as old cars, old clothes, and old records.

Antique collecting is popular all over the world today. Some people buy antiques so they can sell them later for higher prices. Some buy them to show their wealth and good taste. Some collect old objects, such as coins, as a hobby. And some just like the look and feel of beautiful old things.

Antiques come from almost everywhere in the world. Much antique furniture comes from Europe, America, and the Orient (eastern Asia). European and American furniture is often grouped in the general style of the furniture built during a period of years, such as the Regency period in England in the early 1800s or the American Colonial period. The furniture is called by that name. Furniture may also be grouped by the area from which it comes or by the name of the designer—for example, Chippendale or Duncan Phyfe. A piece of Chinese furniture takes the name of the dynasty such as Ming or Tung Chi (a long line of rulers who belonged to the same family) during whose rule the furniture was made.

It does not take expert knowledge or great wealth to become an antique collector. A person may decide to collect old spoons, or perhaps miniature lamps that were once used as nightlights, or old books and maps, or even toys. People can learn as they collect antiques. Libraries, museums, shopkeepers, and antique shows help collectors learn to know different kinds of antiques.

In a way, everyone lives with antiques—the antiques of the future. A hundred years from now, a favorite toy, chair or picture—even this encyclopedia—may be an antique treasure in someone's home or in a museum collection.

▶ ▶ ▶ ▶ **FIND OUT MORE** ◀ ◀ ◀ ◀
Collecting

LEARN BY DOING

What is the oldest thing in your home? Look around and find out. Almost every family has something old—a gold watch from grandfather, an old Bible, a letter from long ago. What was life like when these old things were made?

ANTISEPTIC

Cut fingers or scraped knees should be washed with soap and water to make sure the injury is clean. The soap acts as an *antiseptic* to prevent infection in the break in the skin. The word "antiseptic" comes from two Greek words that mean "against poison." The English surgeon, Joseph Lister pioneered the use of antiseptics in the 1860s. He used carbolic acid to prevent infection during surgery.

Antiseptics, such as soap and other chemicals, kill bacteria (germs) or stop their growth. Hot steam and ultraviolet light are also good at killing bacteria. Bacteria cause swelling, fever, pain, or sickness if they get into the bloodstream. Skin usually keeps them out. An antiseptic stops the growth of harmful bacteria while broken skin is growing back together again.

▲ It is fun to collect only one kind of antique, just as you may collect shells or stamps. Some people collect old watches like this French one. See how it has covers to protect the face and back.

▼ The surgeon Joseph Lister used carbolic acid as an antiseptic spray to disinfect the air during an operation.

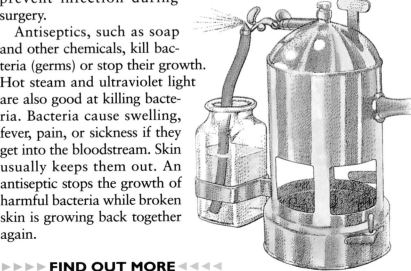

▶ ▶ ▶ ▶ **FIND OUT MORE** ◀ ◀ ◀ ◀
Bacteria, Disease

ANTONY, MARK

SEE CAESAR, JULIUS;
CLEOPATRA

APACHES

The Apaches probably wandered to the southwestern United States from Canada along the eastern flanks of the Rockies about A.D. 1000. They were nomads, with no fixed settlements. The tribe's name was given to them by a neighboring tribe, the Zuni. The Zuni word *Apachu* means "enemy." The Apaches earned their name for they sometimes raided villages of other tribes when food was scarce. In better times, the men hunted buffalo and other game. The women picked wild plants and grew squash and corn. Apache families lived in *wickiups*, houses built of branches. Women owned the wickiups, and both men and women spoke at the tribal meetings.

The Apaches were fierce warriors. The settlers and other Native American people respected and feared their warlike ways. Apache leaders, such as Cochise and Geronimo of the Chiricahua band, terrified settlers. The Apaches fought to preserve their way of life and to protect their lands for almost 40 years after New Mexico became United States territory. They resisted the American settlers until 1886 when the U.S. army captured Geronimo.

About 12,000 Apaches live in Arizona and New Mexico today. Many of these Native Americans live on reservations. Some raise cattle, cut timber, and work in industry.

▶ ▶ ▶ ▶ **FIND OUT MORE** ◀ ◀ ◀ ◀
Cochise; Geronimo; Indian Wars;
Native Americans

APARTMENT

SEE HOUSE

APE

When Americans were getting ready to send men into space, they wanted to be sure that it would be safe. So first they decided to send up an animal as much like a man as possible. They chose a chimpanzee. A chimpanzee is an ape, one of the most highly developed animals.

Apes—together with lemurs, monkeys, and human beings—are members of the order of mammals called *Primates*. The four main kinds of apes are the chimpanzee, the gorilla, the orangutan, and the gibbon. They live in the hot, humid forests of Africa and Asia, and feed mainly on fruits, leaves, and nuts, although some apes steal birds' eggs and others may catch small animals for food.

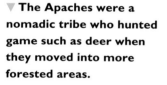

▼ The Apaches were a nomadic tribe who hunted game such as deer when they moved into more forested areas.

The body of an ape is like the human body in many ways. For this reason, apes are sometimes called *anthropoid* ("humanlike") apes. Apes have no tails, unlike most monkeys. They have muscles, nerves, and organs (such as the appendix) that are similar to a human's. Their bones are also like a human's, but their

sea mammal, is as smart. Apes are quick to learn, and they can even be taught to use tools. Some scientists claim that apes are able to learn a simple form of human sign language.

The *chimpanzee,* of central West Africa, is the brightest of all the anthropoid apes, and probably the most popular with humans.

▼ **The orangutan is an ape that spends almost all its time in forest trees.**

arms are longer and their legs shorter. The lower end of the ape's backbone is straight, not curved. This makes it possible for the ape to walk standing up straight, although most apes prefer to walk on all fours.

Another important trait that apes share with humans (and other primates) is the *opposable* thumb. This means the thumb can move in opposition to, or against, the other fingers, so the thumbed hand can hold food and other objects easily. But unlike humans, the ape has opposable thumbs on its feet as well as on its hands.

An ape's skull is thicker than a human's, and its brain is not so large or complicated. Next to a human, the ape is one of the most intelligent of all animals. Possibly only the dolphin, a

▶ **The chimpanzee is the ape most like human beings in some of its behavior.**

▲ **Gibbons are the smallest apes. Their very long arms are adapted for swinging through the trees.**

▼ **The gorilla is the most powerful of the apes. But it is a shy and gentle plant eater.**

Chimpanzees live in bands, or groups, and have a complex social organization. Young chimpanzees are especially playful, and love to show off skills they have learned. Adult "chimps," particularly males, become less playful. A full-grown chimp weighs as much as a grown man but is only about 5 feet (1.5 m) tall. Its face and hands are usually black or pink, and its fur is long and black.

The biggest and strongest of the apes is the *gorilla,* also found in West Africa. The full-grown male gorilla stands up to 6 feet (1.8 m) tall and weighs about 400 pounds (180 kg). Because he is so heavy, the adult male has to stay on the ground when his family climbs into a tree nest to sleep. Gorillas have broad shoulders, powerful arms, and strong jaws. When a male gorilla is in danger, he often tries to scare away his enemy with loud noises, but he usually does not stand up and beat his chest with his fists. Gorillas look fierce but they are really very shy. Of all the apes, only the gorilla is a strict *vegetarian* (vegetable eater) that never eats another animal.

The *orangutan* is found only in Borneo and Sumatra. Its name means "old man of the woods." It spends almost all of its time in trees. The orangutan has a reddish-brown coat, stands about 4 feet (1.2 m) tall, and weighs about 200 pounds (90 kg).

The smallest of the apes is the gibbon. It is much smaller than the other three, which are known as "great apes." The gibbon weighs from 12 to 20 pounds (5–9 kg), and stands from 17 to 39 inches (43–99 cm) tall. It spends much of its time in the trees. It has very long arms and can move very fast, swinging hand-over-hand from branch to branch. On the ground, the gibbon walks upright, balancing its arms over its head, like a small child learning to walk. Seven kinds of gibbon live in Southeast Asia and Indonesia. Many have white, woolly hair when they are born, but the color changes as they grow. Some gibbons, including the *lar* gibbon, keep some of their white coloring, usually around the face and on the hands and feet. The *siamang* gibbon, which is the largest gibbon, is known for its loud cries. Its cries are amplified through a throat sac.

Because of their similarities to humans, apes are among the most fascinating of animals. They have been used extensively in scientific and medical research. Studies of ape societies have also helped our understanding of humans.

Apes are mostly protected in the wild, but there are often problems with poachers. A poacher illegally traps and sells apes. Another problem is the destruction of the apes' habitat. Roads have been built in areas where apes live and land has been cleared for farming. Special reservations are now being set up where the apes can live safely.

▶▶▶▶ **FIND OUT MORE** ◀◀◀◀
Mammal; Monkey

APOLLO SPACE PROGRAM

SEE ASTRONAUT; MOON; SPACE TRAVEL

APOSTLES

From his many followers, or disciples, Jesus Christ chose 12 people to carry on his work of teaching, converting, and healing. These were the *Apostles*, a name that comes from the Greek word for messenger, or somebody who is "sent out." After the death of Jesus, it was the responsibility of the Apostles to spread the Gospel, or "good news" of Christ.

The 12 Apostles were: Simon Peter and Andrew, his brother; James and John, the sons of Zebedee; Matthew, or Levi, the tax collector; Philip; Bartholomew, or Nathanael; Thomas, also called Didymus ("Doubting" Thomas); James, son of Alphaeus (called "the Less" to distinguish him from the other James); Thaddeus, believed to be the same person as Judas, or Jude; Simon "the Zealot"; and Judas Iscariot, the traitor. After the death of Judas Iscariot, his place among the 12 was taken by Matthias. Of the Apostles, Peter, James, and John were especially close to Jesus.

Other followers of Jesus are sometimes called Apostles, including James, writer of the Epistle, as well as Paul and Barnabas. Paul called himself the Apostle to the Gentiles (that is, non-Jews). Like the 12, he claimed to know the truth of the risen Christ and to have been commissioned through him to follow in his work.

All the Apostles of Jesus were sent out on at least two trial journeys to preach and heal. The story of their activities after the death of Jesus is told in the fifth book of the New Testament of the Bible, which is called the Acts of the Apostles. It was written in Greek and, it is said, by Luke, the author of the third Gospel. The first part of Acts tells how the early church was set up among the Jews in Judea; the second part describes the journeys of St. Paul and the founding of the Christian church among the Gentiles.

▶ ▶ ▶ ▶ **FIND OUT MORE** ◀ ◀ ◀ ◀
Bible; Jesus Christ

In the many pictures that have been painted of the apostles, they are often shown with a special sign or symbol that can be recognized. St. Peter, for example, carries keys, St. Andrew is seen with a cross like an X, St. John has an eagle, and St. Matthew, a winged lion.

APPALACHIAN MOUNTAINS

The Appalachians are a long chain of mountains reaching from eastern Canada to central Alabama. These mountains are smooth and low compared with the Rocky Mountains, because the Appalachians are much older and more eroded, or worn down. The highest point in the chain is Mount Mitchell, North Carolina, which is 6,684 feet (2,037 m) above sea level. (See the map with the article on NORTH AMERICA.)

The Appalachians are known by various names in different places. Canada has the Notre Dame Mountains. New England has the Green Mountains and the White Mountains. The Adirondacks lie in New York, and the Alleghenies run from Pennsylvania to Virginia. Virginians and North Carolinians call one range the Blue Ridge Mountains. In Kentucky are the

▼ **Leonardo da Vinci painted this picture of the Last Supper. It shows Jesus with his closest followers, who became Apostles and spread the message of Christianity after Jesus' crucifixion.**

▲ The forest-covered Appalachian Mountains, worn smooth by time, were crossed by explorers and hunters heading West. This is a view of Grayson Highlands State Park.

Cumberland Mountains, and along the North Carolina-Tennessee border stand the Great Smoky Mountains. A footpath, the *Appalachian Trail*, runs along the Appalachian ridges for about 2,000 miles (3,220 km), from Maine to Georgia. It has camping sites and hiking paths.

Many rivers begin in the Appalachians. The Potomac, Delaware, Savannah, and other rivers flow eastward and empty into the Atlantic Ocean. The Allegheny and Monongahela rivers meet at Pittsburgh, Pennsylvania, to form the Ohio River, which flows westward into the Mississippi. These rivers cut gaps through the mountains. Thousands of early settlers traveled through these gaps to the West. The frontiersman Daniel Boone led hundreds of pioneers along the Wilderness Road—from Virginia through the Cumberland Gap to Kentucky, expanding the frontier of the new nation.

▶▶▶▶ **FIND OUT MORE** ◀◀◀◀
Boone, Daniel; Erosion; Mountain; North America; River; Wilderness Road

APPENDIX

SEE DIGESTION

APPLESEED, JOHNNY (1775–1847)

Stories from the days of the pioneers tell of a man who loved apple trees, who spent his life planting apple seeds, tending the plants, and giving away little apple trees. His name was John Chapman, but he became famous as "Johnny Appleseed."

He first got apple seeds from a cider mill in Pennsylvania. He planted them in a garden along the Ohio River. When the seeds had sprouted into seedlings, he gave away the trees to people who were heading west, to plant near their new homes.

Johnny Appleseed became well known on the frontier. He wandered through the wilderness carrying a Bible and leaving pages of it for the pioneers. Native Americans thought anyone who looked and acted like Johnny was protected by the Great Spirit.

Some people thought Johnny was crazy to spend his life planting trees he would not live to see. But for

▲ Johnny Appleseed, the gentle frontiersman who loved to plant apple seeds.

many years after his death, thousands of apple trees from Pennsylvania west through Ohio, Indiana, and Illinois bore fruit.

▶▶▶▶ **FIND OUT MORE** ◀◀◀◀
Pioneer Life

APRIL

"Sweet April showers do bring May flowers." This little poem was written hundreds of years ago. The month of April often does have many rain showers. April is the fourth month of the year and has 30 days. The sweet pea is the flower for April, and the diamond is the birthstone of the month. The word "April" comes from the Latin word *Aprilis*, which means "to open."

April is usually the beginning of

spring in the temperate zone of the Northern Hemisphere. In the far north, the weather is still icy cold. In the Southern Hemisphere, April is the beginning of autumn, a harvest time for grain, not a sowing time as on northern farms.

The first day of April is a fun day—April Fool's Day. The custom of playing silly, harmless jokes on

---

DATES OF SPECIAL EVENTS IN APRIL

1 **April Fool's Day.**
2 **Hans Christian Andersen was born (1805).**
   First movie theater opened in Los Angeles, California (1902).
3 **Pony Express began over a route of 1,900 miles (3,057 km) from St. Joseph, Missouri, to Sacramento, California (1860).**
   Jesse James, the famous outlaw, was killed (1882).
4 **President William Henry Harrison died one month after inauguration (1841), and John Tyler became tenth President.**
5 **Booker T. Washington, black U.S. educator, was born (1856).**
8 **Robert Peary reached the North Pole (1909).**
   United States joined World War I against Germany (1917).
9 **Flower Festival in Japan honors the birthday of Buddha.**
   General Robert E. Lee surrendered to General Ulysses S. Grant, ending the Civil War (1865).
11 **Jackie Robinson became the first black to play in major league baseball when he joined the Brooklyn Dodgers (1947).**
12 **Civil War began at Charleston, South Carolina (1861).**
   President Franklin D. Roosevelt died (1945), and Harry S. Truman became thirty-third President.
   Yuri Gagarin became the first person in space (1961).
13 **President Thomas Jefferson was born (1743).**
14 **Pan American Day.**
   George Washington elected first President (1789).
   President Abraham Lincoln shot by John Wilkes Booth (1865).
15 **President Lincoln died (1865), and Andrew Johnson became seventeenth President.**
   Ship *Titanic* sank in the North Atlantic (1912).
   Chesapeake Bay Bridge-Tunnel (world's longest) opened (1964).
18 **Paul Revere, William Dawes, and Dr. Samuel Prescott made their famous midnight ride to warn American patriots (1775).**
   San Francisco destroyed by earthquake and fire (1906).
19 **Battle of Lexington, Massachusetts, began the American Revolution (1775).**
21 **Spanish-American War started (1898).**
22 **Oklahoma Territory opened up to settlers (1889).**
23 **Saint George's Day, the patron saint of England.**
   Traditional birth date of William Shakespeare (1564).
   First public movie showing took place in New York City (1896).
25 **First shots of Mexican War were fired (1846).**
26 **British colonists made first permanent settlement in America at Jamestown (1607).**
27 **President Ulysses S. Grant was born (1822).**
28 **President James Monroe was born (1758).**
30 **First public television broadcast took place from Empire State Building in New York (1939).**

Sweet pea

Diamond

▲ The symbols of April are the sweet pea and the diamond. A person born in April might wear a diamond birthstone ring.

other people on April 1 began in France in the 1500s. The Christian celebrations of Easter and Palm Sunday and the Jewish festival of Passover often come in April.

▶ ▶ ▶ ▶ **FIND OUT MORE** ◀ ◀ ◀ ◀
Calendar; Easter; Holiday; Month; Passover; Season; Spring

AQUARIUM

An aquarium is a tiny reproduction of a water environment. It can be a beautiful, interesting, and convenient way to study plants and animals that live in water, if it is properly made and cared for.

A successful aquarium must have both animals and plants. Plants give off oxygen and provide food for animals. Fish breathe in oxygen, which comes from the plants, and breathe out carbon dioxide. Carbonic acid—which plants need—is made when carbon dioxide mixes with water. This is a *balanced* aquarium.

The best kind of aquarium is a rectangular glass-sided tank. Most beginners start with 10-gallon (38-liter) tanks.

Making an Aquarium

The three main kinds of aquariums are *freshwater, tropical freshwater, and marine* (saltwater). Each of them needs special care, but some rules are the same for all. Here are some basic steps to follow if you want to set up an aquarium.

(1) Wash sand or gravel and spread a layer about 2 inches (5 cm) thick on the bottom of the tank.

(2) Fill the tank with water. Carefully press some plants into the gravel, tall ones in back, short ones in front. If you buy your fish from a pet store, ask for some good plants to go with them. *Hint*: put a clean piece of paper on the sand or gravel before you pour the water in. This prevents the water from stirring up the sand. Remove the paper—it will float on the top of the water—after the tank is filled.

Half-black angelfish

Neon tetra

Blue ring angelfish

Oranda

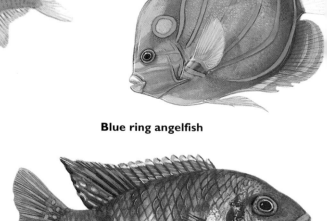

Aulonacara nyassae

▲ A tropical freshwater aquarium can be home to beautifully colored fish of many shapes and sizes. A heater is usually needed for this kind of aquarium because tropical fish need to swim in warm water. It is also important to make sure the tank is not overcrowded.

(3) Be sure that the water temperature is close to that of your fish's natural home. Pet stores sell a special thermometer that hangs inside the tank. Tropical fish need warm water: 75° to 80° F (24° to 27°C). You should buy a heater that fits into the tank and controls the water temperature.

(4) Most aquariums need an *aerator,* a little pump that bubbles air through the water and provides extra oxygen for the fish. Pet stores sell aerators which often include filter systems that keep the water clear and clean.

(5) Place the tank where it gets plenty of light, but not too much direct sunlight. Direct sun can kill plants and cause tiny green algae to grow and spoil the water. You can buy a small electric light that hangs from the top of the tank.

(6) Always try to buy young fish in pairs. Young fish are usually cheaper and healthier than older ones.

(7) Let your aquarium water stand overnight before putting in the fish. Carefully transfer your fish from the plastic bag or container into your tank. Never touch tropical fish with your hands.

(8) Cover the tank with a piece of glass after the fish are inside to keep them from jumping out, to prevent dirt from falling in, and to slow down evaporation. But make sure air can get in by raising the glass just a little.

(9) Always keep the tank very clean. Remove dead fish or rotted plants right away, before they start a disease. Catfish and snails are useful aquarium inhabitants, because they eat scraps. Include a few of these *scavengers.* But snails reproduce very rapidly. Remove young snails, or soon there will be so many that they will destroy the balance of living things. Learn to recognize the tiny, clear ball-shaped snail eggs, so that you can remove the whole cluster of eggs at once. Pet stores also sell tools for cleaning the tank's floor.

(10) Try not to crowd your fish. A good rule is to allow 2 inches (5 cm) of fish length for 1 gallon (3.8 liters) of water. A 10-gallon (38-liter) tank can safely hold ten 2-inch (5-cm) fish, twenty 1-inch (2.5-cm) fish, or one 20-inch (50-cm) fish.

Read more about the kind of aquarium you want, or get advice from a hobbyist or a pet-store owner.

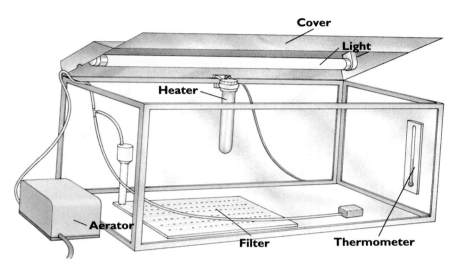

▼ An aquarium should be designed with care. A heater will help to keep the water at the correct temperature and you can check this with a thermometer. A light above the tank helps the plants to stay healthy, but it should not be too bright.

Cover
Light
Heater
Aerator
Filter
Thermometer

Freshwater Aquariums

The simplest aquarium is a freshwater one, in which you can keep small fish from local lakes, rivers, or ponds. Carp, catfish, small bass, crappie, and bluegill are some of the favorites. The fish can be captured in a jar or net and kept in the same water in which they normally live. If you use tap water, let it stand for a few days before you put the fish in. Otherwise, harmful gases in the water can kill the fish.

Carp and catfish eat almost anything, dead or alive. Small pieces of liver or beef are good foods for them. Bass, crappie, and bluegill eat live food, such as earthworms. Never put in more food than the fish will eat in a short time.

A freshwater tropical aquarium is the most popular kind. Watching the colorful fish and the delicate plants in a tropical aquarium is like watching a miniature scene of tropical underwater life. Never use pond or

The ancient Romans dug huge ponds which they stocked with rare and valued fish. But it was the ancient Chinese who first started keeping fish indoors. They bred carp to produce the beautifully colored and strangely shaped goldfish we see today.

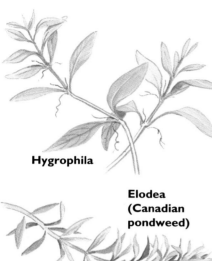

Hygrophila

Elodea (Canadian pondweed)

Cabomba

▲ Aquarium plants help to provide food, protection and a more natural setting for fish. Adequate light will keep plants and fish healthy.

river water in a tropical aquarium, because the tiny organisms that live in pond water will kill the fish. Use tap water, but let it stand for two or three days before you put the fish in. You can use rocks for decoration, but do not use gypsum, alabaster, limestone, or metallic ores. These rocks are poisonous to fish. Safe rocks are quartz, sandstone, petrified wood, and shale.

Many kinds of beautiful fish can be kept in tropical aquariums. Guppies are good fish for beginning hobbyists. Baby guppies are born alive, not hatched from eggs. Guppies can stand some changes in temperature, and they do not get sick as easily as many other kinds of tropical fish. Give all your fish room to swim by keeping one area of the tank free of plants and rocks.

You can buy tropical fish food in most pet stores. Tropical fish also like tiny tubifex worms (available in pet stores) and mosquito larvae. A plastic feeding ring is handy, because it floats on the surface and keeps the food from spreading. The food drops to the bottom in one place and is easy to clean up. Remove any food that the fish do not eat in five minutes, so that it does not rot in the tank.

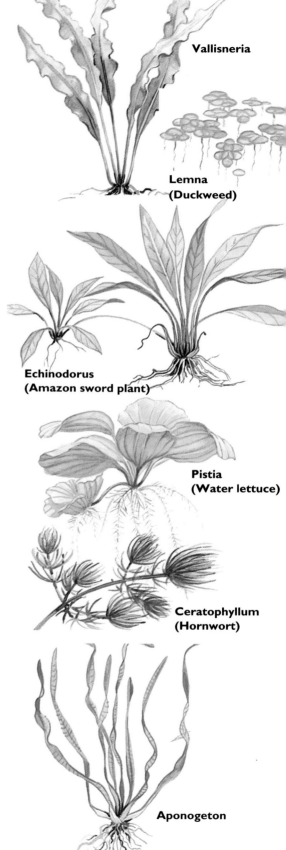

Vallisneria

Lemna (Duckweed)

Echinodorus (Amazon sword plant)

Pistia (Water lettuce)

Ceratophyllum (Hornwort)

Aponogeton

LEARN BY DOING

It is fun to study the water life in your aquarium. Do some kinds of fish hide in plants or near the bottom while others dart everywhere? Are there differences between baby fish that hatch from eggs and those that are born live? Do catfish or other scavengers have different habits from other kinds of fish? An aquarium can give you answers to these questions, as well as many others about the habits and life cycles of water animals and plants.

What kinds of things can you learn about the plants in your aquarium? Why do certain kinds of plants live well under water? What would happen if your aquarium does not have enough light? Or too much light? Do the fish in your aquarium like certain kinds of plants better than others? See what you can learn just by watching the life in your aquarium and see how plants and animals help each other to live under water.

◀ Many species of fish will live happily in a home aquarium. These are Congo tetra, from Africa.

The world's largest aquarium is the John G. Shedd Aquarium in Chicago, Illinois. There are over 300 different kinds of fish on display.

Marine Aquariums

It is possible to set up marine aquariums without living near an ocean, but they are difficult to prepare and maintain. Special all-glass aquariums and artificial sea water are available in pet stores. Water will evaporate from the aquarium, and what is left will become too salty for the fish to survive. So artificial sea water must be added from time to time to keep the correct level of salt in the water.

Sea anemones, sea horses, barnacles, coral, mussels, and small crabs are good animals for marine aquariums. Brilliantly colored tropical fish can also be kept. Sea lettuce and other small ocean plants belong in the aquarium, too. Sea horses and crabs eat small pieces of meat. Sea anemones, coral, mussels, and barnacles eat tiny animals and plants that live in ocean water.

▶ ▶ ▶ ▶ **FIND OUT MORE** ◀ ◀ ◀ ◀
Animal; Animal Homes;
Ecology; Fish; Hobby; Marine Life;
Oxygen; Plant; Pond Life;
Snails and Slugs;
Terrarium; Tropical Fish

AQUEDUCT

SEE WATER SUPPLY

AQUINAS, SAINT THOMAS (ABOUT 1225–1274)

As a young student, Thomas Aquinas was called "dumb ox" by his classmates because he never talked much in class. Yet he grew up to become one of the great teachers, writers, and philosophers of the Middle Ages.

He was born near Aquino, in Italy. At 19, he joined the Dominican order of *friars*, preachers who supported themselves by begging. This angered his wealthy family. While he was traveling with the friars, his brothers carried him off by force and imprisoned him in the family castle for a year. Aquinas did not give up his dream of serving God. In 1245, he began to study in Paris under Albertus Magnus, a famous religious scholar. He followed Albertus Magnus to Germany, but returned to Paris to teach theology.

▼ Thomas Aquinas, a great Christian philosopher.

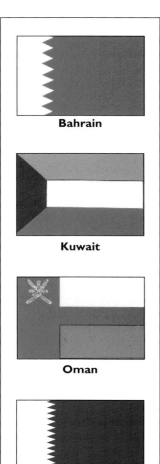

Bahrain

Kuwait

Oman

Quatar

Saudi Arabia

United Arab Emirates

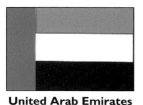

Yemen

His writings on Christian philosophy and teaching have been important in the Roman Catholic Church for hundreds of years. Many of his writings were gathered into a large, three-part book called *Summa Theologica*. His influence on Christian thought has been powerful. Thomas Aquinas was declared a saint in 1323. He was proclaimed a doctor of the church by Pope Pius V in 1567. He is the patron saint of Catholic schools.

▶▶▶▶ **FIND OUT MORE** ◀◀◀◀
Philosophy

ARABIA

Arabia is a large boot-shaped peninsula between the Red Sea and the Persian (or Arabian) Gulf, forming the southwest corner of Asia. It occupies slightly more than a million square miles (2.6 million sq. km), about one-third the size of the United States. The peninsula is divided among seven countries.

Much of the area is barren desert where few people live. The weather is extremely hot during the summer months in the interior and humid on the coasts. On many parts of the peninsula, summer temperatures often reach 120°F (49°C) in the shade. The southern edge of Arabia may receive around 20 inches (500 mm) of rain a year. But in the interior desert, years may pass with no rain at all. Spring and autumn are pleasant seasons. As in many desert regions, days are sunny and warm, and nights, with bright stars and brilliant moonlight, are cool. In winter, December through February, temperatures drop below freezing in central and northern Arabia, but snow usually falls only on the highest areas. In summer the days are burning hot.

In the past, Arabia was best known as a crossroads between the cultures of East and West. It was a center of trade and of learning. The Arab system of numbers (Arabic numerals), on which arithmetic is based, was taken by Western traders to Europe in the 1100s. One of the world's great religions, Islam, originated in Arabia in the 600s. Islam now has more than 550 million followers worldwide. Arabia today is known for its vast deposits of oil, the source of billions of dollars of income to the economy each year.

	Area (sq. mi)	Area (sq. km)	Capital	Currency	Products	Population (thousands)
ARABIA						
Bahrain	240	622	Al Manamah	Dinar	Oil	503
Kuwait	6,880	17,818	Kuwait	Dinar	Oil, chemicals	2,143
Oman	82,030	212,457	Muscat	Rial	Oil, dates	1,468
Qatar	4,247	11,000	Doha	Riyal	Oil	444
Saudi Arabia	830,000	2,149,690	Riyadh	Riyal	Oil	14,131
United Arab Emirates	32,278	83,600	Abu Dhabi	Dirham	Oil	1,881
Yemen	203,850	527,968	Sana	Yemeni, dinar, riyal	Cotton, coffee, hides	11,528

More than 600,000 Muslims from 60 nations visit Muhammad's birthplace, Mecca, every year. Because Mecca is so sacred, only Muslims are allowed to enter the city's gates.

▼ Arabia is the birthplace of Islam, the religion founded by Muhammad.

Arabian History

Sumerian traders crisscrossed Arabia 5,000 or more years ago. They were followed by others: Babylonians, Assyrians, and Persians. Each of these traders left part of their civilization behind in Arabia. Phoenician sailors dropped anchor at bustling Arabian seaports 1,000 years before Christ. And the ancient Romans called the southwest coast of the peninsula *Arabia Felix,* Fertile Arabia. The region was a trade center for frankincense, myrrh, ivory, silk, spices, copper, gold, and jewels.

The prophet Muhammad was born in the city of Mecca (now in Saudi Arabia) in the year A.D. 570. He converted many Arabs, especially the poor and the slaves, to his new faith, Islam, and then set out to carry his teachings to the rest of the world. The religious journey soon turned into a quest for territory.

The Muslims (followers of Islam) defeated Iraq and Persia; spread into India, Africa, Spain, and France; and even took some Byzantine territory. This huge Arab Empire stood until 1258, when Mongols (tribes from eastern Asia) swept through, killing whole populations and leveling whole cities.

Muslim scholars were not interested in the time before Muhammad, and they wrote little or nothing about those thousands of years of Arab history. In fact, some Muslims destroyed early records.

After the year 1258, Arabians lived mostly in poverty and isolated from the West. Their glorious past was little known to Western historians. In the 1800s, archeologists began to find ruins. The ruins of huge cities, long and broad avenues, canals, and dams have been uncovered that tell of an ancient, complex Arabian civilization. And today, even the poorest Arabians have a complicated system of hospitality and social relations that comes from a deep-felt responsibility for every action. This system does not come from the harsh life of the desert, but from an earlier, more prosperous time.

Countries of Arabia

Arabia has been thought of as a distinct geographical area since ancient times. The Romans thought of Arabia as a three-part region:

▼ High, dry mountains surround the fertile tableland of the Yemen.

▲ Arabia is a region of desert. But the oil hidden beneath the desert sand has made Arabia wealthy.

Arabia Felix an independently ruled territory; *Arabia Petrae,* which was ruled by Rome; and *Arabia Deserts* which was ruled by Persia. Until the coming of Muhammad and the founding of the Islamic religion, the history of Arabia was the history of many peoples and many rulers.

From the 1500s much of Arabia was under Turkish rule. But by World War I Turkish control had become weak, and by 1927 the kingdom of Saudi Arabia had come into being. Its founder was King Ibn Saud. In 1938 oil was discovered near Dhahran, on the east coast, and this marked the beginning of a new era for Saudi Arabia. It changed from being a little-known desert kingdom of wandering tribes into one of the world's richest nations.

▲ A souk (covered market) where every commodity is for sale under the same roof—an idea that has only recently reached the West. The two pillars of Islamic life, the market and the mosque (on the right of the picture) are often found near each other.

The other countries of Arabia are much smaller than Saudi Arabia. In the southwest is Yemen, formed in 1990 by the uniting of North Yemen (the Yemen Arab Republic) and South Yemen (the Yemen People's Democratic Republic).

To the east is the independent *sultanate* (a state ruled by a sultan, who is a ruler of a Muslim country) of Oman, which has a fertile coastal strip but a dry and desolate interior. Beyond the Strait of Hormuz lies the Persian (or Arabian) Gulf. Along its shores are the countries of the United Arab Emirates (a federation of seven states ruled by a prince, or emir). The seven are Abu Dhabi, Dubai, Ajman, Sharjah, Umm al Qawain, Fujairah, and Ras al Khaimah. They were formerly known as the Trucial States and, like other states in the Gulf, were protected by Britain until Britain withdrew from the Gulf in the 1970s.

The remaining three independent nations of Arabia are Qatar and Bahrain, both *emirates* (nations ruled by emirs) on the Gulf, and Kuwait, a sheikdom at the northern tip of the Gulf. *(Sheik* is an Arabic word meaning "ruler.")

There was an international effort to free Kuwait after it was invaded by Iraq in 1990. The United States in particular sent large numbers of troops, aircraft, and ships to Arabia. International and Arabian forces freed Kuwait early in 1991.

Oil revenues have helped finance extensive modernization and development of agriculture and industry in all these countries. Only Yemen is not rich in oil.

Arabian Life

Arabs are bound together by a common language, common customs and traditions, and a common faith—Islam. Religion is especially important in the lives of most Arabs. Each Muslim tries once in his lifetime to travel to the holy city of Mecca in western Saudi Arabia.

While some Arabs now prefer to wear Western clothes, many Arabs still wear traditional clothing, designed to protect them from the heat and cold of the desert, even when they live in modern cities. A sheik wears an *abba,* a woolen cloak. A long, white cotton shirt is worn under an abba. The head covering, a *ghoutra,* is a square, cotton cloth

▲ **A Bedouin Arab outside his tent home. Despite the changes in Arabia, many Arabs still lead a nomadic life, herding sheep and goats.**

folded in a triangle and held in place by woolen cords. Arab women commonly wear long robes and veil their faces in most Arabian countries.

Muslim law allows a man to have up to four wives. But nowadays few Arabs take more than one wife.

Women are gaining greater freedom in Arab life, largely because of growing prosperity and better education. In some countries, however, women's freedom is still very limited. In Saudi Arabia, for example, most women may not meet men except for their close relations. Fewer than 1 percent of women work outside the home and none may drive cars. In their homes, many rich women wear gorgeous silks and jewelry.

▶ ▶ ▶ ▶ **FIND OUT MORE** ◀ ◀ ◀ ◀
Arabic; Desert; Islam; Middle East;
Muhammad; Saudi Arabia

ARABIAN NIGHTS

The stories of Ali Baba and the Forty Thieves, Aladdin's Lamp, Sinbad the Sailor, and the Magic Carpet are world famous. Each is from an exciting story in the *Arabian Nights*. This collection of ancient folktales is often called *The Thousand and One Nights*. The stories were first written in Arabic, but the earliest ones came from Persia, India, and Turkey. The author is unknown.

The legend of how the stories were first told is a story in itself. Once upon a time, there was a Persian king, Shariar, who hated women. He would marry a different woman each night. The next morning he would have his new queen killed. He finally chose as his queen Scheherazade, who was as wise as she was lovely.

Every night she told the king an exciting story. But she never finished a tale the same night as she started it. The king was so interested in the stories he let Scheherazade live to tell the endings. By the time 1,001 nights had passed and 1,001 stories had been told, the king liked Scheherazade as much as her stories. She remained his wife and his queen forever.

▶ ▶ ▶ ▶ **FIND OUT MORE** ◀ ◀ ◀ ◀
Arabia; Folklore; Legend;
Magic; Mythology

The world's most powerful cartel is the Organization of Petroleum Exporting Countries (OPEC), made up of Arab nations and others. Since 1973, when OPEC quadrupled the price of oil, it has had a near monopoly in the export of oil.

▼ **The story of Aladdin's Lamp is a favorite tale from the Arabian Nights. According to the story, a genie appeared when Aladdin rubbed the lamp and granted him his every wish.**

The Arabs of long ago made important discoveries in mathematics. Our words "zero" and "algebra" are from Arabic, as are our number symbols such as 1, 2, and 3.

▶ Islamic artists are forbidden to draw people or animals. Instead, they perfected the art of calligraphy, creating beautiful designs and using patterns of flowers and leaves.

▶ An example of Arabic writing. In English it means "In the name of Allah, the gracious, the merciful Allah, there is no other God but him, the Immortal..."

ARABIC

Over 130 million people in northern Africa and the Middle East speak Arabic. The Arabic alphabet has 28 characters formed by dots and curlicues. All the letters stand for consonants, and the shape of each letter depends on its position in a word.

Arabic is written from right to left. The oldest known Arabic writing

dates from A.D. 512, but the exact origin of Arabic is not clear.

The *Koran,* the ancient holy book of the Islamic religion, was written in Arabic. Through the years people studied the Koran and closely copied its style of writing. Written Arabic changed very little. But, as people spoke to each other, spoken Arabic gradually changed until it is now very different from written Arabic. Spoken Arabic also consists of many different *dialects,* where people in different parts of the Arab-speaking world use different words, pronunciation and grammar. Another form of Arabic has developed in recent years. Modern Arabic is used in newspapers, books, radio and television, plays, and movies to discuss new things and ideas that did not exist during the time when the Koran was written.

Arabic belongs to a group of languages called *Semitic* languages. Other major Semitic languages spoken today are Hebrew and Amharic (the Ethiopian language). Ancient Semitic languages that are no longer spoken include Phoenician and Aramaic, the language of Jesus. During the 600s, Islam spread throughout southwest Asia and northern Africa, taking the Arabic language to these areas.

For an idea of how Arabic sounds, imagine a new boy coming to school in Syria. He may say to his classmates, *"Sabah il-khayr"* (pronounced: sah-BAH il KEER), meaning "Good morning." Then he may say: *"Ismi Ahmad"* (is-MEE ah-MAHD), "My name is Ahmad."

▶▶▶▶ **FIND OUT MORE** ◀◀◀◀
Alphabet; Hebrew; Koran; Languages; Number; Written Language

بِسْمِ اللهِ الرَّحْمٰنِ الرَّحِيمِ ۝ اللهُ لَا إِلٰهَ إِلَّا هُوَ الْحَيُّ الْقَيُّومُ ۝

▶ Fisherman catching a sturgeon in one of the artificial lakes created by damming a tributary of the Aral Sea. The Aral Sea once supported a large fishing industry. Fish farms were established in the lakes in an effort to keep the local people employed even though the Sea itself could no longer support the industry. However many people are still unemployed.

ARAL SEA

The Aral Sea is really a lake that lies between the countries of Kazakhstan and Uzbekistan. The lake is shrinking every year. Until 1961, it was the fourth largest in the world, with an area of 24,750 square miles (64,100 sq. km). Now, at 15,000 square miles (40,000 sq. km), it is only the sixth largest.

Because the Aral Sea contained many islands, the Russians named it *Aralskoye More,* Sea of Islands. It was fed by two large rivers, the Syr Darya and the Amu Darya. But water from these rivers has been diverted for irrigation so that farmers could grow cotton, rice, and melons. Now there is not enough water left to feed the Aral Sea. In some years the Amu Darya provides no water at all.

The Aral Sea used to contain 178 kinds of fish, and thousands of people worked in the busy fishing industry. Now the water that was always slightly salty is very salty. Many species of fish died leaving only 38 kinds. The old fishing ports lie many miles from the water, and the land is covered with abandoned boats. The Aral Sea has also split into two lakes. Experts believe that without drastic conservation it will soon vanish altogether.

▶▶▶▶ **FIND OUT MORE** ◀◀◀◀
Caspian Sea; Conservation; Irrigation; Lake

ARBORETUM

SEE BOTANICAL GARDEN

ARCHEOLOGY

Thousands of years from now, something you own may be found by a person called an *archeologist.* It might be a toy, a belt buckle, a dish, or part of your house. By studying the find and testing it, that archeologist may learn a lot about you and how you lived. Archeology is the scientific study of the remains of past civilizations, or ways of life.

The bits and pieces left by ancient peoples can tell archeologists many things. Foundations of buildings and ruins of temples help them know what ancient cities looked like. Objects they find are called *artifacts.* These may be coins, tools, jewelry, or *potsherds* (bits of pottery). Tools, baskets, and pottery all tell something about everyday life. Human bones can tell what ancient people looked like. Animal bones tell what kinds of animals ancient peoples kept, killed, or ate. Archeologists are much like modern-day detectives, eagerly collecting clues and using all their skills to solve a mystery.

Many of the objects discovered will have been cast aside as rubbish by their owners and so are often broken. Complete objects, and sometimes rare and valuable ones, are more often found in graves, where they have been placed for use by their owners

▲ The map shows the Aral Sea as it used to be before the river waters were diverted.

▼ This clay pot was made about 7,800 years ago. The shape and pattern of the pot show that it was made by a skillful potter.

▲ **Archeologists learn much from aerial photography. Seen from above, the outlines of long-hidden ruins, such as this Roman town, are revealed by the camera.**

In many places, as buildings fall down over the centuries, other buildings are put up in the same place. This raises the ground level. People excavating all over modern London have found that today's city is 20 feet (6 m) higher in places than the old Roman town.

▶ **Archeology is a slow, patient science. Workers on a site remove soil very carefully. They set out a numbered grid, marked by strings. Each find is marked to record exactly where it was found. Photographs and drawings are made at intervals as the work goes on.**

after death. Archeologists must always remember that what is left for them to discover may not tell the whole story of earlier ages. Much will have been lost, including objects made of cloth, leather, basketwork, or wood. These are preserved only in very dry or very wet conditions. Unless durable objects have also been left behind, the picture put together by an archeologist will always be incomplete.

Choosing a "Dig"

How do archeologists know where to look for buried cities? In the past, they could only guess by using old maps, legends, the Bible, and ancient historical writings. These gave them hints and some facts as to where to look for remains of ancient civilizations. They might even begin to dig where a farmer had found an old clay pot while plowing a field.

Archeologists today use new methods, such as *aerial photography*. They take pictures from a plane flying over an area thought to have been a lost city. These pictures show shapes that cannot be seen from the ground. Old trenches and walls show up in photographs, hinting where an old city might be buried. When a trench or wall is spotted, the archeologist and a crew go to the place to excavate, or dig. *Underwater exploration* is another way to find things from the past. An archeologist wearing an aqualung can search for sunken treasure in deep waters.

Ancient peoples often built cities on top of older, decayed cities. Many layers underneath each other, called *strata*, which were

made at different times, may be found in one place. Archeologists very carefully and slowly dig down through the layers, keeping accurate records as they go. It is most important that archeologists record exactly where an object was found, and what other objects were found near it in the same layer, in order to know the *context* of a find. Then they can build up a sequence of events in the correct order. If a single object is removed, or a site disturbed, this valuable evidence of the order in which objects were buried will be destroyed.

Archeologists seek the help of other experts to discover all they can about an object. Botanists identify the plants from which preserved pollen grains, seeds, or even charred wood originally came. This can give a picture of what earlier landscapes looked like, what plants were there, what people ate, and what crops they grew. Zoologists can give similar evidence from animal remains. Geologists can find out where building stone came from, for example. Physicists can give a date for objects by using various radioactive dating methods. Many archeologists work for museums, which display the things they find.

Careful records were not always kept when people first became interested in learning about the past. Bits of pots and bones and other ancient objects were often destroyed. Some diggers kept only treasures and pretty things, not knowing how important every artifact might be. Today, however, archeologists preserve every single clue they can find in their study of ancient times.

Relics of life in ancient times have been found all over the world—in the ruins of Pompeii and Troy; in old sailing ships sunk in the Aegean and Mediterranean seas; in the tomb of an Egyptian king—Tutankhamen; in caves near the Dead Sea; in underground rooms built by Native Americans.

Lost cities and civilizations may still lie buried beneath oceans, or covered by centuries of building, or hidden beneath the earth.

▶▶▶▶ **FIND OUT MORE** ◀◀◀◀
Ancient Civilizations; Anthropology

◀ **The body of a Danish woman buried in A.D. 95 was preserved by a peat bog surrounding her.**

▼ **Divers wearing aqualungs can explore ancient wrecks. Sometimes they find long-lost cargoes of wine and oil jars. Occasionally divers find a treasure ship.**

▲ Longbows were developed in England during the 13th century. Skilled archers could use the longbow to fire six arrows a minute.

▼ Shooting for the gold medal in field archery at the 1992 Olympic Games in Barcelona. Archery is a sport requiring a great deal of skill and practice.

ARCHERY

Shooting arrows from a bow is called *archery*. It was invented thousands of years ago for hunting and warfare. Today it is a popular sport. Bows and arrows are dangerous. So a beginner must be taught to handle them correctly and safely by an experienced archer.

Before buying a bow, an archer should know the bow's *draw weight,* or how hard the string must be drawn, or pulled, to shoot the arrow. Draw weights range from 15 to 75 pounds (7 to 34 kg). Bows with low draw weights are for young or beginning archers. Bows from 25 to 45 pounds (11 to 20 kg) are used in tournaments, or shooting contests. Bows today are made of either fiberglass or wood. Bowstrings are usually made of Dacron.

Arrows come in different lengths and thicknesses. An archer picks different size arrows for different purposes. The rear end of an arrow, the *nock,* has a slot that fits around the bowstring. In front of the nock are feathers, called *vanes.* Vanes make the arrow fly straight. The long body of the arrow is the *shaft,* which ends in a metal arrowpoint.

An archer wears a *tab,* or shooting glove, on the hand that grips the bow. An armguard protects his fingers and wrist when the bowstring snaps back as an arrow is shot. A *quiver,* or case, holds the arrows.

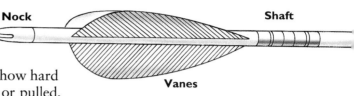

Nock   Shaft

Vanes

A right-handed archer holds the middle of the bow with the left hand. He or she uses three fingers of the right hand to hold the bowstring and arrow. The arrow nock fits between the index and middle fingers. The arrow shaft goes against the left side of the bow. The archer draws the bow, pulling the hand back until the index finger touches the jaw, directly below the eye. This spot on the face is the *anchor point.* The archer aims at the target, and then releases the arrow by relaxing the fingers. Never snap the fingers to release the arrow.

Many nations send archers to world championship competitions and the Olympics. *Target archers* shoot at 48-inch (1.2-m) circle targets, called *butts. Field archers* shoot at much smaller butts. Both shoot from various distances.

▶▶▶▶ **FIND OUT MORE** ◀◀◀◀
Bow and Arrow; Olympic Games; Sports

ARCHIMEDES (ABOUT 287–212 B.C.)

Archimedes is called the "father of experimental science." He was a Greek mathematician and inventor who proved his ideas by experiment. Among other things, he discovered how to use levers and pulleys to lift

heavy objects, and how to pump water uphill.

Archimedes spent most of his life in the Greek colony of Syracuse (Siracusa), in Sicily. He designed war machines for his king. The machines helped the king hold off an enemy invasion for three years, but Archimedes is said to have been killed during the final battle for the city.

The king of Syracuse once asked Archimedes to tell him if his new crown was pure gold. Archimedes thought of how to test the crown when he stepped into a full bathtub and watched it overflow. His body *displaced,* or moved, a certain amount of water. So a crown of pure gold should displace the same amount of water as a chunk of pure gold weighing the same as the crown. Archimedes was so excited by his discovery that he rushed naked from his bath, shouting "Eureka!" (I have found it!) When he performed the test, Archimedes found that the crown displaced more water than the gold chunk, and so was not pure gold. The goldsmith had cheated the king.

▶▶▶▶ **FIND OUT MORE** ◀◀◀◀
Buoyancy; Greece, Ancient; Machine; Physics; Science

🏛 ARCHITECTURE

🎭 Architecture is the art of designing and constructing buildings. The person who does this work is an *architect.* A painter tries to arrange paints in a beautiful way, and an architect does the same with building materials. But architects must do more than design beautiful buildings. They must be able to plan useful buildings, and

they must know practical ways to build them.

In architecture school, students learn artistic design, drawing, and the history of art. They also study engineering and construction methods. After graduating, students enter an architect's office and help in the many jobs necessary to produce complete building plans. At first they are given very simple jobs to do, but as they learn more they are given more responsibility. Finally, they must pass an architecture exam. Then they will be licensed by the state, allowing them to start their own offices.

Buildings today are sometimes so large and complicated that one architect cannot do all the work. These buildings, skyscrapers for example, are usually planned by a team of architects and others in a large office. In addition to the architect for the building and the drafters who help draw the plans, there may be a structural engineer to help design the frame, a mechanical engineer for the heating and air conditioning, a representative on the building site, and so on.

Materials, Moods, and Styles

When an architect first starts to plan a building, he or she must be very sure of what its purpose and size will be. Does a school need a big auditorium? Will families with several children live in an apartment house? Does an airplane factory need extra large rooms and doors? Will an office building serve the needs of different kinds of workers? The architect must also consider the building mate-

▲ Archimedes, scientist and inventor of ancient Greece.

◀ Archimedes is said to have invented this screw machine for raising water for irrigation. By turning the handle at the top, the screw rotates inside a cylinder. Water trapped in the screw is lifted from the lower level to the higher.

▼ The famous lighthouse at Alexandria in Egypt was one of the Seven Wonders of the ancient world. It was built on the island of Pharos and stood nearly 400 feet (122 m) high.

▲ The Temple of Artemis is an example of classical Greek style with its careful arrangement of columns.

▶ The large, curved dome characterizes the Byzantine architecture of Santa Sophia church in Istanbul, Turkey.

▶ Renaissance architecture brought back classical shapes and patterns. The cathedral of Florence, Italy, uses a mixture of Gothic and ancient styles to create a new design.

▼ The Temple of Amon at Luxor. The temples of ancient Egypt were built in honor of great kings and queens.

◀ Ancient Roman aqueducts helped to supply the cities with water. The Pont de Gard, in France, still stands.

◀ Notre Dame, in Paris, France, is built in gothic-style, with pointed arches and stained-glass windows.

◀ The Royal Crescent in Bath, England, is typical of Palladian or Georgian architecture. Classical columns and gardens became a feature of this style.

rials and construction methods available. What materials and workmanship can the client afford? How will steelwork last in a humid climate? Do local fire laws allow wood shingles? What kind of foundation is needed to support a building on swampy ground? All these important questions must be answered.

Good architecture is not only practical. It creates certain moods. A high ceiling makes a room look spacious. A high roof on a house suggests shelter. Heavy, rugged masonry suggests durability and toughness. To give a building the right character or mood, an architect must plan the effect that a building will have from the outside as well as from the inside. Some architects design furniture so that it will match the design of the rooms.

Some architects design the setting of parks or streets for buildings. These *landscape architects* are usually gardeners, too. The way a building looks is called its *style*. A building's style can tell us about the architect's personality, because architects use shapes and colors they like.

Good architecture reflects the needs and way of life of its times. In times when life was easy, architects often used large windows to flood rooms with sparkling light. During hard times, people wanted thick walls and blocky shapes that made them feel safe. Architecture also has changing fashions. Throughout history, there have been numerous fashions, or styles, such as Romanesque, Gothic, Baroque, Contemporary, and so on.

Look at the buildings pictured with this article. How different they all are! Yet they were all designed by architects. They wanted their buildings to be beautiful as well as useful. The spire of the Gothic cathedral soared high above the rest of the town, just as today the tall skyscrapers downtown dwarf other, smaller buildings in the city. Did you know that some of the great European cathedrals took hundreds of years to build?

▼ **The medieval Cutlers' Guildhall at Thaxted, in England.**

The Cutlers' Guildhall in England (above) was built during the Middle Ages. It has a wooden framework with plastered walls. Notice the small windows, and can you see how the second floor is wider than the first floor? Underneath the building is an open space, which was probably used as a meeting place.

Filippo Brunelleschi began the Church of San Lorenzo in Florence, Italy, in 1421. This was during the period called the *Renaissance* (the rebirth of knowledge). Brunelleschi was the first Renaissance architect. His style shows the interest Renaissance people had in science. The walls and ceiling of the church are flat. Straight lines and perfect circles make up the floor tiles, ceiling beams, and windows. The gray marble columns and windows stand out clearly from the white walls. All of these parts of Brunelleschi's design show that he did not want his building to be surprising. Instead, he made his design very regular, so that people could quickly see each part and be impressed by the clear, sharp shapes.

Architects sometimes must finish or remodel old buildings. The Church of St. Peter in Rome was begun in 1506, and several great architects worked on it for over a century. In 1623, Giovanni Bernini, the greatest architect of the 1600s, was asked to complete the church. He worked for more than 50 years. No other architect has ever worked on one project for so long a time. Bernini fitted the work of the earlier architects into his own complicated design, and he made St. Peter's the beautiful and inspiring church we see today.

By the middle 1800s, new materials and inventions were used in designing buildings. As cities became more crowded, architects had to get more people onto less ground space. After the first safety elevator was invented in 1853, architects could save ground space by designing *skyscrapers*—buildings much taller than any built before. Modern steel and concrete are stronger than wood, brick, or stone. So modern

▼ **Filippo Brunelleschi's study of Roman architecture helped him to design the dome of Florence Cathedral. He used vaults, a series of arched bricks or stone, to support the large, curved roof of the dome.**

▼ **Greek columns consist of three main orders: Doric (left), Ionic (middle), and Corinthian (right). Each order had a distinctive decoration and use. Greek columns have been imitated many times since they were first introduced.**

▲ **The Church of San Lorenzo, in Florence, Italy.**

The world's tallest tower is the **CN Tower** in Metro Center, Toronto, Canada. It is 1,822 feet (555 m) high and lightning strikes it almost 200 times every year without doing any damage.

▶ **At 984 feet (300 m) the famous iron structure of the Eiffel Tower dominates the skyline of Paris, France. It was built for the Paris exhibition of 1889 and is named after the architect, Gustave Eiffel.**

Store in Chicago, between 1899 and 1904. This early department store's straight lines and plain walls clearly show it is built of steel and glass. However, thick walls of brick and stone supports hold up the floors and roof.

Another construction method is used for modern steel buildings. All the beams and columns are fastened together into a single framework. Then the walls and floors are hung on this framework, just like paper on a kite frame. Walter Gropius, a German architect, made dramatic use of this construction method. He did not hide the steel skeleton behind solid walls. Instead, in one of his buildings he hung thin glass walls from the roof like a curtain. This building was the *Bauhaus,* an art school that Gropius built in Germany in 1925 and 1926. The glass walls allow daylight to enter every part of the art studio. The steel framework and concrete floors can be seen inside this glass shell. Many offices and factories also have glass walls to let light inside and to let the workers have an outside view.

Le Corbusier, a Swiss architect, helped design the United Nations building in New York. He also built a mountaintop church in France in the 1950s. This concrete church, with its curved roof and walls, tiny windows, and hidden doors, seems to grow out of the ground. Le Corbusier used concrete shapes to express the moods of his buildings—using them to create a mood of safety and trust in a church, for instance.

Ludwig Mies van der Rohe, a German-American, planned even the smallest details of his buildings. His Seagram Building in New York City was built in 1957. Every beam and window is exactly related in size and color to every other part of the

buildings can be much higher than earlier buildings but still be safe. Gustave Eiffel, an engineer, proved that very tall buildings can be made of strong metal. The Eiffel Tower, built for the Paris World's Fair of 1889, and 984 feet (300 m) high, was made of iron.

Modern Architecture

Louis Sullivan, an American architect, felt that tall buildings ought to rise as simple rectangles rather than be complicated in form, as most buildings were in 1890 or even later. He loved ornament, but used it more carefully than previous architects did, to keep the basic design simple. He designed the Schlesinger and Meyer Department

▶ Le Corbusier, a famous modern architect, built the Unite d'Habitation, a large apartment building in Marseille, France. Architecture of the mid 1900s concentrated on a simplicity of style. Le Corbusier's building is made of reinforced concrete and raised on concrete stilts.

▲ The Schlesinger and Meyer Department Store (now Carson Pirie Scott & Company) in Chicago, Illinois, was designed by Louis Sullivan (1856–1924). Sullivan was one of the leading architects of the Chicago School of architecture. He designed some of the first skyscrapers.

▼ The Bahaus Workshop in Dessau, Germany, houses the school of design founded by Walter Gropius in 1919. Gropius designed the workshops for the Dessau campus in 1925. The Bauhaus created a simple, unornamented style of design in all fields, including architecture. Their influence is still widely seen today.

◀ The Art Deco style of the 1920s and 1930s influenced the design of the Chrysler Building in New York City, built in 1929. Art Deco was influenced by the Bahaus school of design. Geometric patterns and sleek shapes were typical of the Art Deco movement. Inside the Chrysler Building, bright color schemes add to the Art Deco impression.

The Lloyds Building in London, England, was designed by Richard Rogers. In order to expose the construction of the building, its heating mechanisms were purposely left on display and cranes were left on the top.

building. The Seagram Building is lively and interesting all the time. During the day, its glass walls reflect the movements of the clouds and city around it. At night, lights and people inside make this office building seem to come alive. Mies van der Rohe influenced many later architects because his designs are so interesting.

Today, as well as experimenting with new styles and construction materials, architects are very concerned about making the right kinds of buildings for people to live, work, and play in.

▶▶▶▶ FIND OUT MORE ◀◀◀◀

Ancient Architecture see Abu Simbel; Acropolis; Pyramid; Sphinx
Architects see Michelangelo; Wright, Frank Lloyd
Design and Construction see Bridge; Building Material, Caisson; Castle; Cathedral; Concrete; Construction; Empire State Building; Gothic Architecture; House; Leaning Tower Of Pisa; Pagoda; Stained Glass; Temple
History see Baroque Period; Renaissance; Rococo Art; Romanesque Art

LEARN BY DOING

An architect has to answer many questions in designing a building. Suppose you try designing a new house for your family. Answer these questions. How can your house be friendly? Quiet? How many rooms does your family need? What rooms? How many bedrooms? Where will the trash be collected? What will the kitchen be like? Will there be a driveway? If you want your house to feel friendly, will you use little windows and heavy, rough stone blocks? If you want it to feel quiet and safe, will you use soft colors and shapes that are not surprising? What materials will you use? Wood? Glass? Plastic? Think about the space around the house. Will you have a garden?

Try making two models of your house, one of clay and one of cardboard. Do the two models feel different to you? What difference does coloring make? All these are questions an architect must answer every time he or she designs a building.

▲ The 110-story Sears Tower in Chicago is the world's tallest building. It was completed in 1974.

ARCTIC

Around the North Pole lies an imaginary line known as the Arctic Circle. Can you find it on a globe? (On globes and maps it is drawn at 66½ degrees north latitude—almost exactly three-fourths of the distance from the equator to the North Pole.) North of this line, temperatures are very low for much of the year. In winter it can be as cold as –90°F (–68°C), though even this is not so cold as at the South Pole. Even in summer the average temperature is no more than 50°F (10°C). Frozen soil, called *permafrost,* always lies below the surface of the land. The region is so cold that trees are dwarfed and in places grow only inches high. Few things can live in this bitterly cold, barren region.

In the Arctic are the northernmost parts of Alaska, Canada, Russia, Norway, Sweden, and Finland, most of Greenland (the largest island in the world), many smaller islands, and the Arctic Ocean. About two million people live within the Arctic Circle. Of these people, some 450,000 are native peoples such as Inuit, Native Americans, and Lapps. The largest Arctic city is Murmansk in Russia.

Filling a Hole

The Arctic regions of North America do not touch those of Europe and Asia. The almost circular space around the North Pole holds the Arctic Ocean. Nearly all year a layer of ice, about 6 feet thick, floats on most of the ocean. This "ice hat" is made up of huge chunks of ice called the *polar ice pack.* The ice is slowly pushed in a circle by ocean currents and winds. The Earth's spin on its axis mainly causes the circular movement of the ocean.

The Arctic Ocean is the smallest of the Earth's oceans. The mean depth of the ocean is about 4,000 feet (1,220 m). The ocean covers 5,440,000 square miles (14,090,000 sq. km), including its many seas and bays. This is about the same size as the continent of Antarctica. The Lomonosov Ridge, an undersea mountain range, has peaks that rise as high as 9,000 feet (2,740 m) from the ocean floor. But the ocean is deep in this region —more than 2,500 feet (762 m) of water cover even the highest peak. Deep basins separate many peaks.

The Arctic Ocean's "hat" of ice is worn a little to one side. In summer it reaches about 1,200 miles (1,930 km) from the North Pole down the Pacific Ocean side of the Earth. But the ice extends only half that distance down the Atlantic side, because warm water from the current called the Gulf Stream reaches northward through the Atlantic Ocean.

> Although the Arctic is a cold place, it is much milder than the Antarctic. The South Pole is a desolate place, covered by ice up to two-and-a half miles (4,000 m) thick. Temperatures at the North Pole are higher because of the sea that is just under the ice. The ice at the North Pole is only 16 feet (5 m) thick.

▶ **A massive castlelike iceberg in the Arctic. Such icebergs form when chunks of ice fall into the sea from the tip of a valley glacier.**

The Arctic town of Verkhoyansk in Siberia holds the record for the greatest range of temperature between winter and summer. It has had a winter temperature of -90°F (-68°C) and a hottest summer temperature of 98°F (36.7°C). Can you figure out this frightening difference in temperature in degrees Fahrenheit?

▶ **The polar bear is a strong swimmer with thick, oily fur. It spends much of its time on or around ice floes, looking for food.**

Some pack ice stays in the Arctic Ocean for years, melting a bit in summer and growing bigger again the following winter. Giant sheets of pack ice buckle and break when they push together. Then one large flat piece of ice, or *floe*, slides up over another. The surface crinkles like a plowed field. Channels, called *leads*, open in the ice sheet. Leads made dog-sled travel dangerous for Robert E. Peary, who led the first trip to the North Pole, in 1909.

Sailors in the Arctic

The period from 1400 to 1879 was one of exploration around the edge of the polar ice pack. Explorers searched for fur-bearing animals and for minerals. They tried to find a "Northeast Passage" that would let a ship sail from Europe to Asia, and a "Northwest Passage" that would allow a ship to travel from the east coast to the west coast of the United States. William Baffin sailed the waters west of Greenland in 1616. The Bering Strait, a stretch of water that separates Alaska and Siberia in Russia, was discovered by Vitus Bering in 1728. Nils Nordenskiöld sailed first through the Northeast Passage (1878–1879), and Roald Amundsen was the first to sail through the Northwest Passage (1903–1906).

The U.S. Navy atomic-powered submarine *Nautilus* became the first ship to reach the North Pole underwater. It traveled more than 1,800 miles (2,897 km) beneath the Arctic ice cap in 1958. The submarine *Skate* became the first to surface at the pole in 1959.

Planes of many countries fly over the North Pole on international

LEARN BY DOING

Fill a shallow saucer almost full of water on a freezing cold winter day. Set it outside on a flat surface. Come back in an hour and take a look. Has ice formed on the water's surface? When ice chunks and chips form, blow them about. See how the ice bunches, piles up, crowds under, and rumples. You are holding a miniature model of the Arctic Ocean and its shifting, drifting ice.

flights. The shortest way between some parts of North America and Asia is over the Arctic Ocean. There are weather stations and defense installations in the Arctic.

Cargo ships plow through the Northeast Passage each summer. They sail along the coast of Siberia from Norway. Ice breakers clear channels in the ice. Few ships break through the Northwest Passage in northern Canada, although an oil tanker, *Manhattan,* navigated this route in 1969. Vast oil deposits have been discovered in the Alaskan Arctic, and a pipeline across Alaska was completed in 1977.

There are increasing worries about the environment in the Arctic. Much pollution reaches the Arctic, drifting in the air and in ocean currents. A number of countries have signed pacts to help protect the Arctic environment.

▶ ▶ ▶ ▶ **FIND OUT MORE** ◀ ◀ ◀ ◀

Alaska; Amundsen, Roald; Bering, Vitus; Byrd, Richard E.; Hudson, Henry; Lapland; North Pole; Northwest Passage; Peary, Robert; Polar Life; Tundra

◀ **The Ptarmigan is an arctic bird that has feathered feet to help it conserve heat. It becomes snow white in winter to camouflage it against the snow.**

MAJOR EVENTS IN THE ARCTIC	
330 B.C.	Pytheas discovered Iceland.
A.D. 982	Eric the Red discovered Greenland.
1610	Henry Hudson discovered the strait and bay later named after him.
1728	Vitus Bering discovered the strait later named after him.
1878–79	Nils A. E. Nordenskiöld was the first to sail through the Northeast Passage.
1903–06	Roald Amundsen was the first to sail through the Northwest Passage.
1909	Robert E. Peary led the first expedition to reach the North Pole.
1926	Richard E. Byrd was the first man to fly over the North Pole.
1957–58	Scientists participating in the International Geophysical Year studied many aspects of the Arctic. Over 300 scientific stations were set up in the Arctic to study, among other things, the weather, the ice cap, and the water of the Arctic Ocean.
1958	*Nautilus,* a U.S. atomic submarine, sailed under the Arctic ice cap.
1959	*Skate,* a U.S. atomic submarine, surfaced through the ice at the North Pole, the first ship ever to do this.
1969	*Manhattan,* an enormous oil tanker, was the first large commercial ship to navigate the Northwest Passage.
1977	*Artika,* a Soviet ice-breaker, reached the North Pole.
1986	A U.S./Canadian expedition reached the North Pole traveling on the ice without air support. It was the first to do so since Peary.

▼ **Most of Greenland lies within the Arctic Circle. The short Arctic summer brings out many tundra plants, which bloom quickly in the long, sunny days.**

ARGENTINA

Capital city
Buenos Aires
(9,968,000 people)

Area
1,068,302 square miles
(2,766,889 sq. km)

Population
32,880,000 people

Government
Federal republic

Main products
Meat and meat
products, wheat,
textiles, leather,
machinery

Unit of money
Austral

Official language
Spanish

▼ **Argentina's pampas, or plains, are ideal for ranching cattle, as well as growing wheat.**

ARGENTINA

Argentina is the second largest country in South America. With its grassy *pampas* (vast, treeless, grassy plains), its snow-capped Andes Mountains, and its wild, windy southern plateau, it is a large, beautiful country of contrasts.

About one-third of the Argentine people live in and around Buenos Aires. It is the largest city and most important port in South America. From there, the pampas spread out, fanlike, for 300 to 400 miles (480 to 640 km). Argentina's economy depends almost entirely on the rich, fertile soil of the pampas. Raising beef cattle is its main industry. Argentina is one of the world leaders in production of beef and hides. Wheat, cotton, and flax are also grown on the pampas. Argentina is now one of the greatest wheat-producing areas of the world. In the 1800s, nomadic cowboys, called *gauchos,* herded cattle over the unfenced pampas. But in the late 1800s, a few rich men bought up the grazing lands and fenced in the pampas to raise cattle on huge ranches called *estancias.* The old way of life of the gauchos is gradually disappearing.

Northern Argentina is mostly the *Gran Chaco,* a partly swampy and forested lowland. Southern Argentina is known as *Patagonia,* a dry, windswept plateau region with some forests and grasslands. The climate in the south is harsh, with heavy rainfall and violent winds.

Most of the Indians who live in Argentina live in Patagonia, where sheep raising is the main occupation. Cattle cannot feed on the coarse grasses here. Some of the world's largest sheep ranches are on the island of Tierra del Fuego at Argentina's southern tip. Argentina has an oil

industry, and its factories produce textiles, chemicals, and machinery. About three fourths of the country's people live in the cities and towns.

The highest mountain in the Western Hemisphere, Mount Aconcagua (22,834 feet/6,960 m), is in the Argentine Andes Mountains, which separate Argentina from Chile. The main industries in the mountains are fruit growing, mining, and wine.

Juan Díaz de Solís, a Spanish navigator, claimed Argentina for Spain in 1516. The Spanish soon conquered the Indians, hoping to find their gold and silver. Spain ruled Argentina for nearly 300 years. General José de San Martín, the Argentine national hero, helped Argentina win independence

in 1816. From 1946 to 1955, the president was Juan Domingo Perón, whose wife Eva was a prominent figure in the government. Perón and his third wife, Isabel, ruled again briefly in the 1970s. The military has taken control of the government at various times. In 1982, Argentina went to war with Great Britain over the disputed Falkland Islands. The war led to the downfall of the ruling military government, and elections were held in 1983.

► ► ► ► **FIND OUT MORE** ◄ ◄ ◄ ◄
Andes Mountains; Buenos Aires; Perón, Juan and Eva; South America; Spanish History; Wheat

ARISTOTLE (384–322 B.C.)

One of the greatest philosophers of all time was Aristotle of ancient Greece. He was the student of another great philosopher, Plato. Aristotle joined Plato's school in Athens when he was 18. He stayed there until Plato died, 20 years later.

Aristotle became well known as a philosopher during those years. In 342 B.C., King Philip of Macedonia called Aristotle to teach his son, Alexander, who would later be called Alexander the Great. Aristotle returned to Athens after seven years in Macedonia. Alexander, who had since become king, gave Aristotle money to set up his own school, the *Lyceum*. Aristotle studied, taught, and wrote for 12 years. Then Alexander died. The people of Athens did not like Alexander, and—because Aristotle was his friend—they did not like Aristotle. Aristotle had to leave Athens. He died the following year.

Aristotle studied and wrote about every subject known to the Greeks. Much of his writing was for his students, but only a few of his works have survived. He developed the sciences of logic and physics. His ideas about zoology, politics, ethics, and literature are very important. People all over the world still read his writings.

Aristotle taught that people should act on what their study of life convinced them was right. He said the good of all was served when each person did something about what he thought and believed.

► ► ► ► **FIND OUT MORE** ◄ ◄ ◄ ◄
Alexander the Great; Ancient Civilizations; Greece, Ancient; Philosophy; Plato; Socrates

▲ **Aristotle, ancient Greek philosopher and teacher.**

ARITHMETIC

Arithmetic is the oldest and simplest branch of mathematics. To understand what arithmetic is, we should look at how it developed. The invention of money was an important reason for the development of arithmetic. The merchants of ancient Asia, for example, bought and sold expensive goods. They had to be able to add and subtract large numbers easily and accurately.

A large part of arithmetic in those times was learning how to use an *abacus*. This simple device helped a person add or subtract long lists of numbers quickly and easily.

The ancient Greeks also knew the uses of arithmetic. The word "arithmetic" comes from the Greek word *arithmos*, which means "number." For the Greeks, arithmetic had two parts. The Greeks knew all the rules for adding and subtracting, like the Asian merchants. However, they were also interested in numbers themselves. They divided numbers into many different groups. Some of these groups are easy to understand.

For example, any number that can make a pair or be divided by two, such as 2, 4, 6, 8, 10 and so forth, is called an *even* number. All other numbers: 1, 3, 5, 7, 9 and so forth, are called *odd* numbers. Some kinds of numbers are more difficult to under-

> Aristotle was one of the first persons to state that the world was round. But he wasn't correct in everything he said. He declared, for instance, that a heavy stone would fall to the ground more quickly than a light one. Everyone accepted this until Galileo proved it wrong two thousand years later.

▼ **John Napier, the Scottish mathematician, invented logarithms. In 1617, he explained how small rods or "bones" could be used to multiply or divide.**

The Roman way of writing numerals is still used today. It used seven symbols (I, V, X, L, C, D, M) and was based on the idea of grouping in fives. The system was a good one, but it had two problems: sometimes the numeral was very long—3,867 would have been written MMMDCCCLXVII; also it was impossible to multiply and divide using Roman numerals.

▼ This ancient Egyptian papyrus dates from 1650 B.C., but it was copied from an even older papyrus written between 1849 and 1801 B.C. Arithmetic has been used to solve mathematical problems for thousands of years. This papyrus contains problems for students just like those we do in school today.

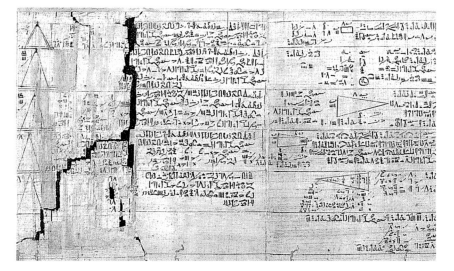

stand. An interesting kind are *perfect* numbers. With every perfect number, if you add up all the numbers that divide it evenly, their sum is the number you started with. Six is a perfect number. The numbers that divide six evenly are 1, 2, and 3; and $1+2+3=6$. Another perfect number is 28, because $1+2+4+7+14=28$.

Another important advance in arithmetic came around A.D. 750, when *Arabic numerals* were first used. Arabic numerals are the numbers we use today. They are the symbols "1, 2, 3, 4, 5, 6, 7, 8, 9, 0." When we use these ten numerals, we can write even the largest numbers by combining the symbols in different ways. Many ways of writing numbers existed, but they were all complicated and hard to use. Because Arabic numerals use only ten symbols, it is fairly easy to add, subtract, multiply, and divide.

Roman numerals are another way to write numbers: 1 = I, 2 = II, 3 = III, 4 = IV, 5 = V, 6 = VI, 7 = VII, 8 = VIII, 9 = IX, 10 = X. Try adding these Roman numerals together without changing them into Arabic numerals: VI + VIII + IX = ??? See how much easier it is to use Arabic numerals.

Arithmetic still needed quick methods to solve problems. The ways to solve problems using Arabic numerals were not discovered until the 1700s. Many mathematicians

helped to discover the rules to solve problems.

What Is Arithmetic?
Arithmetic is the study of how to add, subtract, multiply, and divide numbers. These are called *operations*. People who study arithmetic learn how to perform the four operations: *addition, subtraction, multiplication*, and *division*. Each of these operations has a sign: addition (+), subtraction (-), multiplication (×), and division (÷).

ADDITION. Two apples and three apples equal a total of five apples. This is a simple example of addition. Addition takes two numbers and combines them to get a third number, which is their sum. Here are more complicated examples of addition:

382	(Addend)	342
+513	(Addend)	+234
895	(Sum)	???

Each number above the line, 382 and 513, is called an *addend*. The number below the line, 895, is called the *sum*. In our example, each *digit* (numeral) in the sum can be found by adding the two numbers above it. The process is sometimes more difficult, however, when bigger numbers have to be added. Can you fill in the sum where the question marks are?

SUBTRACTION. In subtraction, you want to know the difference between two numbers. How much larger is one number than another? It is easy to see that three apples is the difference between two apples and five apples, or 5 - 2 = 3. More complicated examples are:

589	(Minuend)	682
-352	(Subtrahend)	-211
237	(Difference)	???

The large number on top, 589, is called the *minuend* in this subtraction problem. The number below it, 352, is called the *subtrahend*. The answer, 237, is called the *difference*. You can get the answer by subtracting the 3, 5, and 2, in 352, from the numbers just above them. Find the difference in the other problem. It is easy to see if your answer is correct in a subtraction problem. The subtrahend and the difference add up to the minuend number if the answer is correct. In this problem, 352 + 237 = 589, so 237 is the right answer. Was your answer to the other problem right?

MULTIPLICATION. Imagine a merchant in ancient Asia. A trader comes into the merchant's tent and offers the merchant eight chests. Four silver bowls are in each chest. How many bowls are there altogether? One way to solve this problem would be to add 4 to itself 8 times. If you did this, you would find there are 32 silver bowls. But it is easier to multiply the eight chests by four bowls in each chest:

```
   8      (Multiplicand)
 x 4      (Multiplier)
  32      (Product)
```

In this example, 8 is the *multiplicand* and 4 is the *multiplier*, which tells how many times to add 8 to itself. The answer is 32, which is the *product*. What would be the product if the merchant had 2 chests containing 6 bowls each?

DIVISION. If the trader has 32 silver bowls and 8 empty chests how many bowls can he put into each chest? He can solve this problem by dividing the number of chests (8) into the total number of bowls (32).

```
        4        (Quotient)
   8 ⟌ 32
 (Divisor)  (Dividend)
```

The *divisor* is 8. The *dividend* is 32, and the *quotient* is 4, the answer. It is easy to check whether you have done a division problem correctly. The divisor (8) multiplied by the quotient (4) will equal the dividend (32). The answer shown is correct in this case, because 4 x 8 = 32. Whenever a number divides evenly into another number, it is called a *factor*. In this example, both 4 and 8 are factors of 32, because they divide evenly into the number 32.

People use certain kinds of numbers to add, subtract, multiply, and divide. The numbers we used in all our examples are *whole numbers*. Whole numbers are made by adding 1 to itself any number of times. Whole numbers are called *integers*—2, 14, 137, and 1,000,000 are all integers. There are many other kinds of numbers, however.

Among the most important numbers are *fractions*. For example, a pie can be cut into four equal pieces. Each piece is a fraction, or part, of the whole pie. Each piece is one-fourth of the whole pie, or ¼. If the pie is divided into three equal parts, each piece is ⅓, or one-third, of the whole pie. The number above the line in a fraction is called the *numerator*. The one below the line is the *denominator*. Fractions can be added, subtracted, multiplied, and divided—although sometimes it is difficult to do so.

Using *decimal numbers* is a quick way to write fractions. Decimal numbers are used because they are easy to multiply and divide. The fraction ¼ is 0.25 when written as a decimal number, for example. The period in a decimal number is called a *decimal point*. The fraction ¼ is the same as 25 ÷ 100. Any fraction can be turned into a decimal fraction by dividing the numerator by the denominator.

▶ ▶ ▶ ▶ **FIND OUT MORE** ◀ ◀ ◀ ◀
Abacus; Decimal Number; Euclid; Mathematics; Number

QUIZ

1. What is an ordinal number?
2. If you put $5 in the bank and it earns 5 cents interest every day, how much money would you have after 30 days?
3. Susie can usually walk to school in 30 minutes, but last Tuesday she overslept and had to run all the way to get there on time. She got there ⅓ faster than normal. How long did she take?
4. On Thursday Susie left extra early so she could stop by her friend Sharon's house on the way. All in all it took Susie 1½ times as long as usual to get to school. How long did she take?

(Answers on page 256.)

COMMON FRACTIONS AND THEIR DECIMAL EQUIVALENTS

⅛ = 0.125
¼ = 0.25
⅓ = 0.333
½ = 0.5
⅔ = 0.666
⅞ = 0.875

ARIZONA

Arizona, nicknamed the "Grand Canyon State," or "Apache State," is the sixth largest state in the United States. It has become one of the nation's fastest growing areas, despite the state's deserts, mountains, and dry, empty highlands. Arizona has a rugged beauty and a healthful climate. The sun shines much of the time. The air is dry and clear. It is seldom hot in the highlands. Since the 1950s more and more people have moved to Arizona.

▲ The Grand Canyon was carved out of rock over the past 6 million years by the Colorado River, which flows through it.

The Land

Arizona is in the Southwest. It lies on the border of Mexico and is between California and New Mexico. The highest parts of Arizona are in the north and east, where rough highlands reach more than one mile (1.6 km) above sea level. Rivers have worn canyons out of the rock over the ages.

In central Arizona are the San Francisco Peaks, which are extinct volcanoes. They are more than 12,000 feet (3,650 m) high in places. Their tops are white with snow most of the year. Forests cover the mountainsides in central and northeastern Arizona. Pines and other trees grow there because the mountains receive enough water in the form of rain and snow. Parts of the highlands are dry most of the year. But they have rain at times. In spring and summer, grass comes up on the dry highland.

Southwestern Arizona is different from the rest of the state. It is low. There are mountains here, but most of them are not so high as those farther north. The yearly rainfall here is very slight. Most of southwestern Arizona is desert or almost desert. Farm crops need to be irrigated in order to grow. The only wild plants are those that need little water, such as the creosote bush, mesquite, yucca, and cactus. Cacti can store water for lengthy periods. Many kinds of cactus grow in southwestern Arizona. The largest, the saguaro, takes about 100 years to reach its full height of 50 feet (15 m).

History

Native Americans probably lived in the region 20,000 years ago. About A.D. 100, the *Hohokam* people (ancestors of the *Papago* and *Pima* tribes) settled in the Gila River valley. They were pit dwellers who built extensive irrigation ditches for their fields. The *Mogollon* people settled in the east, the *Anasazi* settled in the north.

The *Pueblos,* descendants of the Anasazi, built many-storied houses of sun-baked stone and clay. Many of these cliff dwellings, called *pueblos,* still stand. In the 1300s, the *Apaches* and *Navajos* moved into the region, and later the *Hopi, Yuma,* and other tribes came. The Native Americans lived mostly by farming, not hunting. Corn was their main food.

In the early 1500s Spaniards in

STATE SYMBOLS

◀ The cactus wren is Arizona's state bird. It gets its name from its cactus habitat.

▶ The state seal was adopted in 1911. Its symbols relate to important economic activities.

◀ The state flower is the flower of the saguaro cactus. It is white and flowers on top of the cactus or its branches.

◀ The palo verde, the state tree, is a shrublike tree that grows in hot, arid climates.

ARIZONA

Capital and largest city
Phoenix (983,403 people)

Area
113,909 square miles
(295,023 sq. km)
Rank:
6th

Population
3,665,228 people

Rank:
25th

Statehood
February 14, 1912
(48th state admitted)

Principal river
Colorado River: 690 miles
(1,110 km) in Arizona

Highest point
Humphreys Peak:
12,633 feet (3,851 m)

Motto
Ditat Deus
("God Enriches")

Song
"Arizona"

Famous People
Cochise, Geronimo,
Zane Grey, Helen Jacobs,
Barry Goldwater,
Frank Lloyd Wright

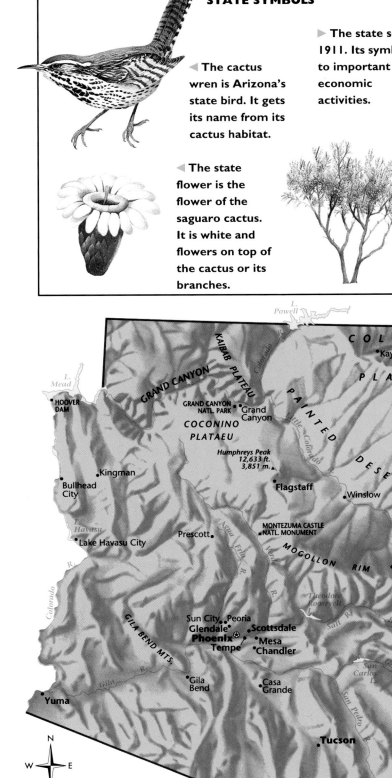

▲ **A view of Phoenix, the state capital of Arizona.**

New Spain (later known as Mexico) became interested in the country to the north. Estevanico, a black man, guided Marcos de Niza, a Spanish priest, to the Arizona area. In 1540, Marcos guided a Spanish expedition led by Francisco Coronado. The Spaniards explored a huge area. They made Arizona and much other land part of New Spain. Spanish priests later tried to convert the Native Americans to Christianity.

Many of the Native Americans of Arizona rebelled against rule by the settlers more than once. In 1821, Mexico (which included Arizona) won independence from Spain. Warlike northern Native Americans then became even bolder. After an uprising in 1827, many settlers gave up their homes in Arizona. They moved farther south in Mexico.

Arizona did not remain part of Mexico for long. The U.S. won a war with Mexico in 1848. Most of what is now the southwestern U.S., including Arizona, became part of U.S. territory through the peace treaty with Mexico in 1848 and the Gadsden Purchase in 1853.

Pioneers moved into Arizona. They took over the Native American's land for farms and ranches. Cochise, Geronimo, and Mangus Colorados led the Apaches in many raids against the settlers. U.S. troops under General George Crook waged war against the Native Americans (1882–1885).

The Native Americans finally surrendered. The federal government set up areas called *reservations*. Even today Arizona has more than 174,000 Native Americans living on or near reservations. Seven in every hundred Arizona citizens are Native Americans, although they are outnumbered by Hispanic Americans.

Arizona became the 48th U.S. state in 1912. More and more people settled there to raise cattle, operate mines, or enjoy their retirement years.

Natural Resources

Arizona's minerals include copper, gold, silver, lead, uranium ore, oil sands, and zinc. The state is especially rich in copper. More than one-half of all the copper mined in the United States comes from Arizona. Another natural resource is timber from the forests on Arizona's mountain slopes.

More land could be farmed if there were more water for irrigation. Arizona tries to make the best possible use of its limited supply of water. Much water falls in the Arizona mountains in the form of snow. The snow begins to melt in the spring. To catch the water, dams have been built across rivers. The mighty Hoover Dam was completed in 1936. The water backs up behind the dams and forms lakes. Canals and ditches take the water from the lakes to farms. Farmers also use water from underground wells that have not been pumped dry.

▶ **Saguaro National Monument, near Tucson, is home to many kinds of cacti. The famous saguaro, however, towers above the other species.**

Working in Arizona

The leading industry of Arizona is making machinery, including airplane parts and electronic equipment. Mining is the second biggest business. Raising cattle and growing irrigated crops are also important. Cotton is the principal field crop in Arizona. But Arizona's third largest industry is not agriculture. It is tourism.

By far the most spectacular place to see is the Grand Canyon of the Colorado River. The canyon is actually a river valley carved out of the rock. It is more than 200 miles (320 km) long and from 4 to 18 miles (6 to 29 km) wide. It is a mile or more deep in some places. As sunlight changes during the day, the rocky walls change their colors.

Two other unusual sights in Arizona are the Petrified Forest, made up of ancient tree trunks that have turned to stone, and the Painted Desert, with its strangely colored stone and sand. Other tourist attractions are the Lake Mead recreation area, the rebuilt London Bridge at Lake Havasu City, and Meteor Crater.

▶ ▶ ▶ ▶ **FIND OUT MORE** ◀ ◀ ◀ ◀
Coronado, Francisco; Estevanico; Exploration; Grand Canyon; Mexico; Painted Desert; Petrified Forest

ARKANSAS

The state of Arkansas was given the official nickname "The Land of Opportunity" in 1953. People have used the rich natural resources of the state to make a better life for themselves. Arkansas's businesses, factories, farms, and mines have thrived through people's effort.

Arkansas is a southern state. It lies near the center of the South. The Mississippi River flows past its eastern edge. Missouri is north of Arkansas, Louisiana is south of it, and Oklahoma is to the west. Texas is at the southwest corner of Arkansas.

▲ **Little Rock is the state capital and largest city in Arkansas.**

The Land

Arkansas's land is partly high, partly low. Its highlands are in the northwest. The rest of the state is made up of low plains. The valley of the Arkansas River divides the high lands in two. The Boston Mountains, north of the river, are the roughest part of a big high area, the Ozark Plateau. A good place to see the Boston Mountains is at Devil's Den State Park. Huge, strangely shaped rocks can be seen in this park. The Boston Mountains are too steep to farm. They have been left mostly as forestland.

The Ouachita Mountains, located south of the Arkansas River, are also forested. The name "Ouachita" comes from a Native American word meaning "Good Hunting Grounds." Little Rock, the capital of Arkansas, is in the Ouachita foothills, low hills rising to the mountains. Westward, the Ouachita Mounains get higher. Some are over 2,500 feet (760 m). The Ouachita River flows through the center of the region.

Much good farmland lies in the Arkansas Valley. Farmers raise crops near the Arkansas River. The land is fairly level there, and the soil is better. Cattle graze where the hillsides are too steep for plowing and harvesting.

When French explorers arrived in the area that is now the state of Arkansas they found a Native American tribe that called itself the Akansa or Akansea. The French spelled the name in various ways, but soon they settled on the spelling Arkansas. When the United States bought Arkansas from France in 1803, the Americans took over the French pronunciation of the name. They spelled it Arkansaw because that was the way it sounded. Finally, in 1881, the state legislature declared that the spelling was to be Arkansas but the name was to be pronounced ARK-unsaw.

ARKANSAS

Capital and largest city
Little Rock
(175,795 people)

Area
53,104 square miles
(137,539 sq. km)
Rank: 27th

Population
2,350,725 people
Rank: 33rd

Statehood
June 15, 1836
(25th state admitted)

Principal river
Arkansas River:
250 miles (402 km)
in Arkansas

Highest point
Magazine Mountain:
2,823 feet (860 m)

Motto
Regnat Populus
("The People Rule")

Song
"Arkansas"

Famous People
William J. Clinton,
James W. Fulbright,
Douglas MacArthur,
Winthrop Rockefeller

STATE SYMBOLS

◀ **The state seal** shows symbols of industrial and agricultural wealth.

▶ **The state tree** of Arkansas is the pine, which grows in abundance all over the state.

▲ **The apple blossom, the state flower, belongs to the rose family. Apple seeds and trees were brought over to the United States by early European settlers.**

▼ **The mockingbird is the state bird of Arkansas. The mockingbird gets its name from its habit of mimicking other birds.**

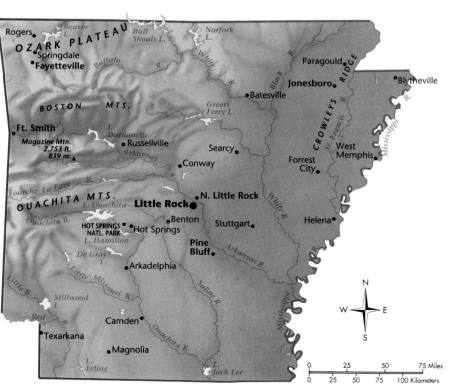

The best Arkansas farmland is in the rolling plains of the lowlands. Most of the soil there is very fertile. The Ozark and Ouachita regions have usually silty and sandy soils.

Arkansas has an in-between climate. Winters are not cold. The average January temperature is 38°F (3°C). Summers are warm. The average temperature in July is 80°F (27°C). Winds blow mostly from the southwest, bringing warmth to Arkansas. Spring starts early and fine autumn weather lasts until December. The result is a long growing season. Plenty of rain falls throughout the year. Autumn, the time for harvesting crops, is the driest season.

Natural Resources

Because Arkansas has many rivers, lakes, and springs, it has an abundant water supply that is convertible into hydroelectric power. The state's most important mineral resources are oil, bauxite, bromine, and natural gas. The state produces most of the nation's bauxite—the source of aluminum. Also, there is plenty of stone, gravel, and sand.

Forests cover almost three-fifths of the state. Oak, hickory, pine, ash, gum, and other trees are cut for lumber or wood products.

Arkansas is noted for its wildflowers, ferns, and herbs. There are American bellflowers, yellow jasmines, orchids, and water lilies.

Wildlife is a natural resource. Among the animals in the state's forest are deer, bears, foxes, muskrats, minks, and many kinds of birds. Arkansas is on the Mississippi flyway, a broad north-south path along which millions of birds migrate each spring and fall. Eastern Arkansas is an important resting place for wild ducks and geese in the fall, when they are flying south.

History

Spanish soldiers under the command of Hernando de Soto were the first Europeans to enter what is now Arkansas. They came seeking gold in 1541 but did not make a settlement. More than 100 years passed before Europeans again came to Arkansas. This time they were French explorers. The Native Americans whom the French met were northern people who had traveled south down the Mississippi River to reach this pleasant land. They called themselves "Downstream People." The French never learned to say the Native American word for "Downstream People." "Arkansas" was as close as they could come.

◄ **Hot Springs National Park attracts nature lovers from all over the country. The hot springs waters are thought to be helpful in treating certain illnesses.**

What is now Arkansas became part of the huge Louisiana territory, claimed by France. The U.S. government bought the whole territory from France in 1803, for $15 million. Arkansas became a state of the Union in 1836.

Arkansas had over 400,000 people by 1860. More than one-quarter of the population were black slaves. Arkansas joined other southern slave states in breaking away from the U.S. in 1861 and forming the Confederacy. The Confederate States were defeated in the Civil War, which lasted from

1861 until 1865. All slaves were freed after the war.

Since the Civil War, Arkansas has had many struggling farmers. The continual planting of a single crop, cotton, wore out the soil in many areas. The average farmer lacked the money to buy the machinery, fertilizer, and other equipment needed for modern farming. Poverty and the Great Depression drove hundreds of families out of the state in the 1930s and 1940s.

Working in Arkansas

In 1955 Arkansas set up the Industrial Development Commission to try to bring in more industry. The Arkansas River Development Program improved navigation on the Arkansas River, built new flood control dams and new water-power plants to supply cheap electricity. Many new factories were attracted to the state. Thousands of new jobs became available. Today, over half of the state's people live in towns and cities.

Manufacturing earns more money for Arkansas than farming. Important products are foodstuffs, lumber, paper, and electrical machinery. Farming is still very important in the state. Soybeans are the crop that brings in the most money for farmers. Chickens, rice, cattle, and cotton are also grown.

Thousands of tourists visit Arkansas each year. Many of them go to Hot Springs National Park to swim, boat, fish, and camp. Some people find that bathing in the water from the hot springs improves their health. Visitors can hunt for diamonds in the only diamond mine in the United States, located near Murfreesboro. Other attractions for visitors vacationing in the state include Blanchard Caverns, Eureka Springs, and Dogpatch U.S.A.

▶ The armadillo has a coat of scaly armor for defense. It can also burrow quickly to escape its enemies.

▶▶▶▶ **FIND OUT MORE** ◀◀◀◀
Civil War; Louisiana Purchase;
Mississippi River; Reconstruction

ARMADILLO

Strange defenses have helped certain animal species survive. The armadillo's armorlike covering is its protection. The armadillo is a long-tongued mammal whose chief food is insects. It is fairly small but heavy. The name *armadillo* means "little armored one" in Spanish.

An armadillo is born with a soft, leathery covering. The special skin of armor plates, or bands, hardens, except at the joints, as the animal grows. The armor coat may cover the legs and tail. Armadillos are timid creatures and burrow quickly to hide when they are attacked. The armadillo's armor sticks up above ground to plug up its burrow. The *Three-banded armadillo* can roll up completely into a hard ball.

About 20 different species of armadillo live in South and Central America. The smallest is the *Fairy armadillo,* a tiny pink animal. The largest is the *Giant armadillo.* It grows up to 4 feet (1.2 m) long. The *Nine-banded armadillo* of Mexico and the southwestern United States spends sunny days in its burrow. It hunts insects and snakes at night. This armadillo has the amazing ability to swallow air so its intestines inflate. It can then float across a river like a rubber raft.

▶▶▶▶ **FIND OUT MORE** ◀◀◀◀
Animal Defenses; Anteater; Mammal;
Skin; Sloth

ARMENIA

Armenia is a western Asian nation with a long and troubled history. It lies on the Armenian Plateau, part of the Caucasus Mountains that lie between the Caspian and the Black seas. Turkey is its neighbor to the west.

Armenia's location is at one of the crossroads between Europe and Asia. Trade routes passed through the Caucasus Mountains for centuries. Many nations fought to control this area, making Armenia a battleground. Armenians have been ruled by the Persians, Greeks, Romans, Arabs, Turks, and Russians.

Armenia has a dry climate, with long, cold winters. But the good soil means that farming is very important. The hot summers help Armenian farmers grow large amounts of cotton. There are also many fruit orchards and vineyards, mainly along the Aras River. Cattle and sheep are raised in the mountains.

The ancestors of the Armenians settled in the Armenian Plateau about 2,500 years ago. The nation that they established, now called historic Armenia, was much larger than today's independent state. It extended well into what is now Turkey. For a short time it extended from the Caspian Sea all the way to the Mediterranean.

Despite being ruled by different empires, the Armenians kept their own identity. They were the world's first nation to accept Christianity as their official religion, early in the A.D. 300s.

By the mid-1600s Armenia was divided. Western Armenia was ruled by the Turks as part of the Ottoman Empire and it is still part of modern Turkey. Persia (now called Iran) controlled eastern Armenia. Russia took over this region in 1829.

Turkey and Russia had long been enemies. Turkey saw how those people in Russian Armenia had better living conditions. They worried that Armenians in Turkey would side with Russia in World War I. The Turkish government deported many Armenians. More than a million died during a dangerous journey into Syria.

At about the same time, the people of Russian Armenia went through major changes. The Russian Revolution of 1917 ended the rule of the Russian emperors, called *czars,* and created the Soviet Union. In 1918, Russian Armenia declared its independence. But independence lasted only two years. Armenia was forced to join the Soviet Union rather than be conquered by Turkey.

Once again Armenia faced stern rule by foreign powers, this time the communist rulers in Moscow. Conditions improved after the 1950s and by the late 1980s Armenia, like other Soviet republics, was given more power to govern itself. In late 1991 the Soviet Union came to an end and Armenia joined 11 other former Soviet republics to form the *Commonwealth of Independent States.*

▶ ▶ ▶ ▶ **FIND OUT MORE** ◀ ◀ ◀ ◀
Azerbaijan; Russian History

◀ **A Tang dynasty (A.D. 618–907) model of an Armenian trader. The Chinese preferred to let foreigners handle their trade and Armenia, at a crossroads between East and West, profited by this.**

ARMENIA

Capital city
Yerevan

Area
11,306 square miles
(29,280 sq. km)

Population
3,300,000 people

Government
Republic

Main products
Copper, zinc, aluminum

Unit of money
Ruble

Official language
Armenian

© 1994 GeoSystems, an R.R. Donnelley & Sons Company

ARMOR

In ancient times, soldiers fought with swords, spears, knives, and bows and arrows. Most battles were fought hand-to-hand. Soldiers needed protection that they could wear or carry. This was known as *armor*.

The earliest armor may have been coats made of layers of heavily quilted cloth. Ancient Egyptians and Assyrians wore this kind of armor as early as 300 B.C. Homer, the Greek poet, described armor made of leather and bronze, worn during the Trojan War.

Armor often had three main parts: a helmet, a jacket, and leg coverings. A metal helmet was worn to protect the soldier's head. The helmet had a chin strap so it would not fall off. There were two types of jackets, both of which came down to the knees. A jacket made of *chain mail* had many small rings of metal hooked closely together, like a knitted sweater. Chain mail was used in Europe 2,000 years ago. It was light and flexible, so the wearer could move easily. The second type of jacket was made of leather or padded cloth with overlapping strips of metal sewn to it. This plate-type material was stronger than chain mail, but heavier. It was developed by

▼ Examples of styles of armor. Each part of a suit of plate armor had a special name.
1. visor
2. breastplate
3. gauntlet
4. couter
5. cuisse
6. greave
7. sabaton

Plate armor, around 1500

Norman, around 1100

Saracen, around 1200

Crusader, around 1200

ancient Egyptians and Persians. Both types were popular as long as armor was used. Soldiers often wore both kinds of jackets, one over the other. *Greaves* were pieces of leather or metal that strapped around the soldier's leg below the knee.

Soldiers also carried shields. The first shields were probably made of wood covered with leather. Later shields were made of metal. A shield had a strap on the inside that fitted over the soldier's arm. It also had a hand grip so he could hold it firmly. The best shields were thick enough to protect a soldier, but light enough to be carried in battle.

Knights in Armor

In the late part of the Middle Ages, from about the 1400s to the 1500s, Europeans used another kind of armor called *Gothic* armor. This armor was a metal suit that covered the whole body, except for small slits in the helmet. Even the gloves were made of armor. Each suit had to be especially made for the person who wore it. Gothic armor was worn in battle mainly by knights. Their horses often wore metal armor too.

A knight's main weapon was a *lance,* a long, sharp, heavy spear that fitted into a holder on the armor and rested on the saddle. He charged with his lance pointed at enemy knights. Of course, the other knights had lances too. Each wanted to knock the other down. Other weapons often used by knights were swords, hammers, and maces or spiked clubs. Armored warriors carried heavy metal shields to defend themselves. If a knight were knocked off his horse, the armor was so heavy that he had a hard time getting up again. One rule of battle was that a knight could be captured while lying on the ground, but he had to be well treated as a prisoner.

Full suits of armor were made for knights with horses, but lighter models were also made for foot soldiers.

Owners of suits of armor paid much money for them. Some armor had beautiful designs and jewels.

Friendly knights fought each other in sporting contests in times of peace. They entertained crowds and kept in practice for war. These contests were called *jousts,* or tournaments. At the jousts, knights wore extra heavy armor and used lances without points. The knight who knocked the other off his horse won.

In the early 1500s, crossbows and, later, guns made suits of armor useless. Bullets could pass through armor, and in a gunfight, armor was too heavy anyway. However, armor is still used today. Soldiers and police officers on riot patrol often wear helmets and bulletproof vests made of steel plates sewn to cloth. Construction workers and fire fighters wear *hard hats* to protect them from falling objects. In sports, race car drivers, motorcyclists, football players, hockey players, polo players, and baseball umpires wear various kinds of armor to keep them from getting hurt badly.

Armored Vehicles

From the 1800s warships were strengthened with steel armor plate to protect them against gunfire. During World War I armored cars and tanks made their first appearance on the battlefield. During World War II airplanes, too, were armored.

Today, civil armored cars are used to transport gold, money, and payrolls. They are designed to withstand attacks by criminals, and provide protection against gunfire and poison gas.

▲ Mail armor was made by cutting rings from thick wire (1). The rings (2) were closed up (3), the ends flattened (4), and holes drilled (5). Then they were fastened with a rivet (6) after linking.

The thickest armor ever used was on the British battleship *Inflexible,* built in 1881. It was 24 inches (61 cm) thick. Teak planks behind gave a total thickness of 42 inches (107 cm).

▶ In 1969, Neil Armstrong became the first person to set foot on the moon.

ARMSTRONG, LOUIS (1900–1971)

Louis Armstrong was a showman as well as a great jazz musician. His many concerts in Europe were such triumphs that he was called one of America's most popular goodwill ambassadors.

Armstrong was born in New Orleans, Louisiana. He learned to play the trumpet in an orphans' home in that city. As the music called *jazz* developed, Louis Armstrong, nicknamed "Satchmo," helped it grow. In 1922, he went to Chicago. There he won fame in King Oliver's band. Armstrong started his own band in 1925. He played his horn freely and wildly, often *improvising,* inventing new melodies as he played. Sometimes he used his gravelly voice to shout meaningless sounds to the music—a style called *scat singing.*

Louis Armstrong's trumpet improvisation became the envy of other jazz musicians. Armstrong went to New York in 1929, where he led many bands. He made many records, including some of his own jazz compositions. Appearances in films and television and at jazz festivals made him known all over the world. In 1966, he won an award for best jazz musician at the First World Festival of Negro Arts, in Dakar, Senegal. He told the story of his start in jazz in his autobiography, *Satchmo: My Life in New Orleans.*

▼ Louis Armstrong became one of the first jazz musicians to perform improvised solos.

ARMSTRONG, NEIL (1930–   )

"That's one small step for a man, one giant leap for mankind." With those words, Neil Armstrong climbed from the Apollo lunar module *Eagle* and became the first person to stand on the moon, on July 20, 1969. This was the high point of his flying career, which began when he was 16.

Neil Armstrong was born in Wapakoneta, Ohio. He earned his Navy wings at 19. He flew 78 missions in the Korean War. As a test pilot, he flew an X-15 rocket plane to 207,000 feet (63 km) at 3,818 miles an hour (6,144 km/hr).

The National Aeronautics and Space Administration (NASA) picked Armstrong and eight others to be astronauts in September 1962. In March 1966, after almost four years of training, Armstrong and David Scott flew Gemini 8 and performed the first successful docking of two vehicles in space. Armstrong's next mission was as commander of the Apollo 11 moon landing. One year after the Apollo 11 flight with Edwin Aldrin and Michael Collins, Armstrong went to work with NASA in Washington, D.C. He now works as a consultant in the private sector.

▶▶▶▶ **FIND OUT MORE** ◀◀◀◀
Brass Instruments; Jazz

▶▶▶▶ **FIND OUT MORE** ◀◀◀◀
Astronaut; Moon; Space Travel

ARMY

An army is an organized group of soldiers who are trained to fight mostly on land. During a war, the main job of an army is to defend the homeland against invasion or to invade and gain control of enemy territory and the enemy army. Even after a war is over, an army may stay and control the territory it has conquered.

Ancient Armies

People have always fought one another, but they have not always had professional armies. The earliest wars were short battles between tribes, usually over a piece of land

Civil War (Union)

War of 1812

that both tribes wanted. Every man who was able and willing to fight picked up a club and some stones and joined the battle. After the battle was over, the men returned to their everyday lives.

The first professional armies developed with the growth of great civilizations in the Middle East, Egypt, and China. The soldiers of a professional army are paid to be in the army full-time, whether a war is on or not. When there is no war, they practice using their weapons and study techniques of warfare.

Ancient armies were first made up of *infantry*, or soldiers who fight on foot. The Assyrians are thought to have been the first to use horses in battle. They had charioteers and *cavalry*, or soldiers who fight on horseback. Today, the name "cavalry" is sometimes used for soldiers who operate tanks and armored cars, and even for airborne fighters.

In the city-states of ancient Greece every young man had to serve in the army for a time. This practice is known as *universal service*. In Sparta, boys began their military training at the age of seven. They continued to

World War II

Modern colonel, U.S. Infantry

▲ Some of the uniforms soldiers have worn since Congress created the Continental Army in 1775.

serve in the army until they were 60. Compulsory service in the army existed in ancient Persia and Rome and in Europe during the Middle Ages. France adopted the modern military *draft* system, or *conscription*, in 1792. Napoleon formed huge French armies from *draftees*. Today, most nations in time of war use the draft to raise armies. Some nations, like Israel, draft men and women.

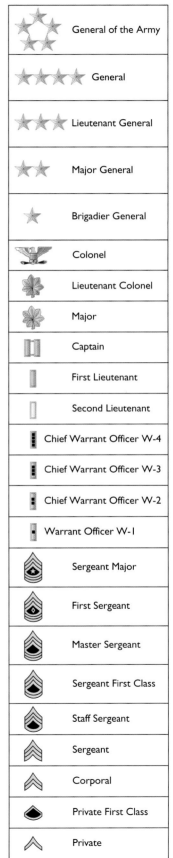

SOME ARMY INSIGNIA

	General of the Army
	General
	Lieutenant General
	Major General
	Brigadier General
	Colonel
	Lieutenant Colonel
	Major
	Captain
	First Lieutenant
	Second Lieutenant
	Chief Warrant Officer W-4
	Chief Warrant Officer W-3
	Chief Warrant Officer W-2
	Warrant Officer W-1
	Sergeant Major
	First Sergeant
	Master Sergeant
	Sergeant First Class
	Staff Sergeant
	Sergeant
	Corporal
	Private First Class
	Private

▲ Soldiers of the French Foreign Legion march down a street in Djibouti, once part of France's colonial empire in Africa.

▶ The U.S. Army insignia is based on the Great Seal of the United States. It was adopted in 1778.

▼ The U.S. Army Medical Corps is essential support service for the Army.

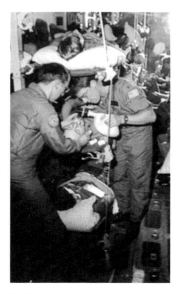

An army is usually made up of soldiers who fight for their own nation. But sometimes a nation hires foreign soldiers called *mercenaries*. They promise to be loyal to the nation that hires them. Probably the most famous mercenary army of all time was the French Foreign Legion, started in 1831. It fought for France all over the world.

What Makes a Good Soldier

There are six important things that make soldiers fight well: strong leaders, efficient weapons, adequate supply lines, good training, firm discipline, and high morale.

The leaders must know how to plan and fight wars well so the soldiers will trust their orders, even in times of great danger. The weapons must be at least good enough to give the soldier a fair chance in fighting the enemy. Many modern weapons are very complicated, and the soldiers must be carefully trained in how to use them properly.

Discipline makes a soldier obey orders and keep fighting, even when he is tired, frightened, or does not understand fully the reasons for the orders. It comes from good training and inspiring leadership.

High morale or *esprit de corps* often makes the difference between winning or losing. *Esprit de corps* means the soldier has confidence in his leaders, himself, and in the other people on his side. It means pride, too, and a strong belief in a cause. In the American Revolution, the Continental Army held together in the terrible cold winter at Valley Forge because of high morale.

The U.S. Army

Before the American Revolution, each colony had a *militia* made up of men of all ages who were prepared to fight if needed. Militiamen made up the backbone of the Continental Army when it was formed in 1775 under the leadership of George Washington. One command, or branch, of the Army is still called the Continental Army. It is in charge of the ground defense of the United States. Other combat commands are stationed in the Atlantic, the Pacific, Europe, South Korea, and Alaska. Some commands are joint operations with other services. For example, the Army and the Air Force work together in the Tactical Air Command.

Those who go into the Army are volunteers. After passing certain health requirements, they go through basic training to learn about the Army, their weapons, and simple field activities. They then go into special training for combat with helicopters, tanks, or missiles, for example, or for support work. The support troops include people who work with supplies, communications, research, or the business of running the Army. Some volunteers learn to be officers, or leaders.

The U.S. Army has a women's branch called the Women's Army Corps (WAC). The women are volunteers also. They do not serve in combat but provide much support that releases men for more hazardous jobs. Women also serve as nurses and medical workers.

The reserves and the National Guard back up the regular U.S. Army. Reserves are servicemen and servicewomen who train for a short time every year, so that they are ready for active duty in case of war. Each state organizes its own National Guard, which is controlled by the governor. The reserves and the National Guard are called into the regular army to fight only by order of the President with the approval of Congress.

Armies today have other important jobs besides fighting wars. One is riot control. A riot happens when a crowd of people becomes violent. Sometimes a riot is so big that the local police cannot stop it. The army is ordered to help. Another job of an army is to help people in case of natural disasters such as floods, hurricanes, forest fires, and earthquakes. Armies have often been called on to help build roads and dams, to dredge rivers, or to aid in health projects, such as malaria control.

▶ ▶ ▶ ▶ **FIND OUT MORE** ◀ ◀ ◀ ◀
Air Force; Armor; Eisenhower, Dwight D.; Fortifications; Guerrilla Warfare; Guns and Rifles; MacArthur, Douglas; National Guard; Tank; United States Service Academies; Weapons

ARNOLD, BENEDICT

SEE ALLEN, ETHAN; TREASON

ART

Who can say what art is? Or even what good art is? Surely art is doing, making, creating something of your own. It gives you a good feeling inside that you have done something new and exciting. Art can take many forms. It can be writing a story or playing a song on the piano that sounded just right. It can be making a finger painting that is bright and swirly. It can be digging deep into a blob of clay and bringing about a pleasant shape. Art for you might be dancing out a story you made up. It could be acting out a fairy tale with some friends or reading a special poem out loud to people who care. What is art for you? It must be something you like to do that satisfies you.

Art of Different Times and Places
New arts spring up everywhere. All peoples of the world have developed some art forms. Many children who live out in the country come to know birds very well and have often learned to make beautiful birdcalls. That is a kind of art. Others draw and paint pictures of the birds they

◀ **U.S. soldiers were greeted by jubilant French civilians in Paris in 1944. The United States had helped to drive German troops from France near the end of World War II.**

▶ **This sculptor fashions animal figures out of clay. Clay is easy to mold and can be baked hard in an oven called a kiln.**

The largest art gallery in the world is the Winter Palace and Hermitage in St. Petersburg (formerly Leningrad), Russia. There are nearly 3 million works of art and you would have to walk about 15 miles (24 km) to see them all.

see. This art is better known. In the mountains of Switzerland many years ago, people made many kinds of bells. That finally led to the art of the Swiss bell ringer who played tunes on bells. Maybe you can make up your own new art!

Some children take part in art at the professional level. The Vienna Choir Boys, for example, travel about the world giving concerts. They sing beautiful music by the greatest composers and perform in front of thousands of people. The oldest boys in the choir are 13 or 14. The youngest are about 8 or 9.

Children from many parts of the world who like to paint have had their paintings shown in the international exhibits sponsored by the United Nations Educational, Scientific, and Cultural Organization (UNESCO) at the U.N. in New York and in many foreign lands.

Sometimes, talent for a certain art runs through a family. There are fam-

▼ *Hoosick Falls in Winter.* **The paintings of Grandma Moses are of happy and carefree days in the countryside. She did not begin painting until she was 76.**

ilies who enjoy singing together. Pop star Michael Jackson and his brothers sang together for some years. Other families have all played musical instruments and have had family orchestras. Some families, like the Wyeths, have several painters in them. The Sheen/Estevez and Douglas families have a number of actors and actresses.

You may develop an art any time in your life. In 1961, an old woman died in New York State at age 101 years. She was called "Grandma Moses" (Anna Mary Robertson Moses). She was a hard-working woman who reared a large family and kept a big farm going until she was old. She did sewing and embroidery. But her hands became stiff with arthritis, and she couldn't sew anymore. Then someone gave her a box of paints. She began painting pictures of life on the farm in the olden days. People liked her pictures and began to buy them. By the time she was in her eighties, she was famous. Before she died she had lived a whole new life with the art she found in her old age.

Some forms of art are not always very well accepted when they are first introduced. But later they come to be highly prized. This was true of the French Impressionists of the late 1800s. People often laughed at these young artists' paintings and wouldn't let them into art exhibitions. Now the Impressionists' work is highly prized. Pierre-Auguste Renoir (1841–1919) was a French Impressionist. It is hard to imagine that *A Girl with a*

Watering Can was not liked when it was first viewed!

Some talented artists are not discovered until after they die. The poet Emily Dickinson is very famous now, but no one in her hometown of Amherst, Massachusetts, thought of shy Emily in the white dress as a poet. After she died, hundreds of poems in her handwriting were found in her dresser drawers, though she had only six poems printed when she was alive. She wrote poetry all her life, not to get attention from the world, but because she loved creating poetry.

Art Among Groups

Groups of people sometimes produce certain kinds of art. One talent seems to spark another. An unusual religious group called the *Shakers* lived more than 200 years ago in a community in New York State. The craftsmen in this group made beautiful furniture. Their designs were simple but handsome and the woodworking was very well done.

▲ *A Girl with a Watering Can* **was painted by the French Impressionist painter Auguste Renoir. It hangs at the National Gallery of Art, Washington, D.C., Chester Dale Collection.**

Today Shakers have all but disappeared. But Shaker furniture is prized in museums as beautiful art. Who were the Shaker carpenters? No one knows their names, but working together they made furniture that is lasting art.

In the days of slavery in the South, blacks created the art of the *spiritual*—a song of worship that is great American music—songs like "Swing Low, Sweet Chariot" and "Little David, Play on Your Harp." Why did spirituals develop? Who wrote them? No one can say. Slaves were forbidden by law to read and write. They were given little chance to learn to play musical instruments. But nothing could stop them from singing. They sang as they picked the cotton, lifted heavy loads, and carried out a thousand hard chores in the hot sun. And they created an art by making up songs—the words and music of which they could not write

◀ **Art can be useful and beautiful. The Shakers were a religious group who made simple and elegant furniture.**

down. It was great art, from an unexpected place.

Fine Arts and Applied Arts

In our times, arts that are intended just for beauty are called *fine arts*. These include sculpture, painting, music, dance, drawing, literature, architecture, and drama. Which one is your favorite now? You might enjoy trying every one of the fine arts at some time in your life.

The principles of design and beauty in the fine arts are put to use in the *applied arts*. People now feel that everything that is built

▼ A wood carving of a reclining figure, by the British sculptor Herry Moore (1898–1986).

or made in a factory should be done with good design. This is *everyday art*. Lovers of everyday art say that the bridge you cross on your way to school should be beautiful to look at. The school that you walk into every morning should be pleasing to the eye. Your desk should be made to look graceful as well as be comfortable. The dishes your family uses should be pretty to look at and big enough to hold your meal. Everyday art goes further—to *beautification*. Why should you pass an ugly dump of wrecked automobiles on your way to school? That dump can be cleaned up, and trees planted there. Beauty can grow by the roadside for you to enjoy every day.

In the future, you may work at jobs only three or four days a week. Machines will help people do some of their work. You will have more free time than any people in history.

The most valuable painting in the world is thought to be the *Mona Lisa* by Leonardo da Vinci, which hangs in the Louvre in Paris. It is quite small—only 30$\frac{1}{2}$ by 21 inches (77 by 53 cm), and it is said that King Francis I of France once had it hanging in his bedroom.

You will have more time for the arts. Very often the arts you like as a child become the arts you love as a grown-up. What arts would you choose as hobbies? The important thing is that you enjoy them. Your art should say, "This is me. This is what I think." And only you can say what the arts are for you.

▶▶▶▶ **FIND OUT MORE** ◀◀◀◀
Architecture; Art History; Dance; Drama; Drawing; Literature; Music; Painting; Sculpture

ARTERY

SEE CIRCULATORY SYSTEM

ART HISTORY

People throughout history have loved drawing, painting, sculpture, and other visual arts. In fact, some people say that the most important test of a civilization is the art it produces. Many civilizations that have vanished completely are known only for their beautiful art. Art often recorded important events in a culture.

The most ancient art was done by the people of the Old Stone Age. Their art has been found in caves in France and Spain and several places in Africa. Look at the painting of a bison. It was found deep in a cave at Altamira, Spain. See what bright colors the artist used, earth colors made from different colors of soil. The artist carried the paints deep into the cave and, working by torchlight, painted this picture of a dying bison on the wall. The bison has long since disappeared from Spain. We know almost nothing of the people who painted the picture, exactly when they lived, or what they thought. Yet, we can look at this picture now, about 30,000 years after it was painted, and be thrilled with its color and life and the story it tells us.

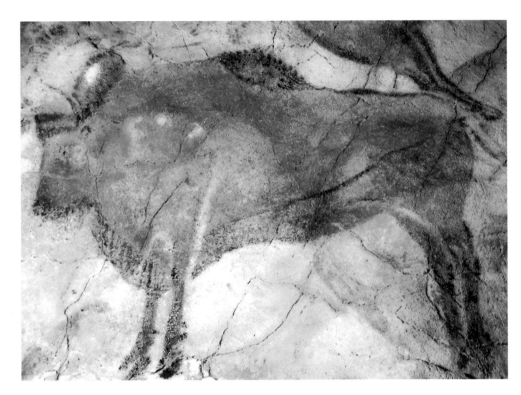

◀ Some of the oldest-known works of art are cave paintings, like this one of a bison from Altamira, Spain. Such Stone Age paintings may have had some magical meaning for the hunters who painted them.

Ancient Art

Thousands of years passed between the time of the cave paintings and the dawn of *recorded* time, after written language had been invented. The Egyptians were among the earliest people to use written language. They built a remarkable civilization beside the Nile River. Most of their art history has been found in their famous pyramids, built as tombs for their rulers. The Egyptian rulers spent years getting ready for their deaths. Their tombs were decorated with art to accompany them on their journey into the next world.

At the same time, the Chinese were producing beautiful art of the Bronze Age. Handsome bronze vessels made during the *Chou* dynasty (the ruling family from about 1766 to 1122 B.C.) are outstanding examples of ancient art. Chinese artists produced great art work for the next 2,000 years.

The greatest culture of the ancient world was in its glory in the years from 460 to 300 B.C. The Greeks were perhaps the most artistic people in world history. They designed beautiful buildings. They had long since mastered the working of bronze. They also made clay pottery of great perfection. Their bronze and marble sculpture has had a longer period of greatness. The marble statue (see picture on next page) of *Hermes*, the messenger god, is by Praxiteles, a great Greek sculptor who lived from about 390 to 330 B.C. Hermes is holding the infant god Bacchus. The statue has beautiful curves, and the figure is standing in a relaxed manner.

Christianity changed the lives of people, as it spread in the first few hundred years after Christ. Religion became the subject of most art. The painting of Christ (see picture on

◀ The ancient Chinese made beautifully carved, bronze vessels to cook sacrificial food for their dead ancestors.

The biggest "old master" painting is in the Doge's Palace in Venice, Italy. It is *Il Paradiso* by Tintoretto and measures 72 feet 2 inches by 22 feet 11½ inches (22 m by 7 m). There are 350 people in the picture.

▶ *The Birth of Jesus* **by Giotto, the Italian Renaissance painter.**

▼ *Hermes* **by Praxiteles, the ancient Greek sculptor.**

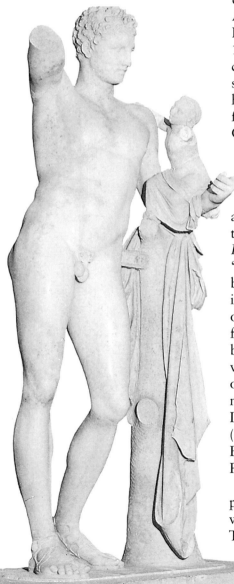

this page) is by an unknown artist of the late days of the Roman Empire, about A.D. 600. It shows Christ as a young man, in the way the people of the early church saw him.

Compare this picture of Christ with a painting of the baby Jesus and Mary done several hundred years later. The artist, Giotto di Bondone (about 1276–1337), was born near Florence, Italy. He decorated the little Arena Chapel in Padua, starting in 1304. The painting above is from the chapel. See how he arranged a few solid-looking forms in space? Note how different his style was from the flat style of the earlier painting. Giotto made a great breakthrough in painting. He developed depth.

The Renaissance

Giotto and his glorious work came at the beginning of a very exciting time in European painting—the *Renaissance*. The word means "rebirth." The rebirth of the arts was brought about by a renewed interest in ancient arts. Florence, Venice, and other Italian cities became wealthy from world trade. An amazing number of talented artists lived and worked within a period of 200 years or so. Three of the greatest—the masters of the High Renaissance in Italy—were Leonardo da Vinci (1452–1519), Michelangelo Buonarroti (1475–1564), and Raphael (1483–1520).

Michelangelo was a sculptor and painter. One of his greatest projects was painting scenes from the Old Testament on the ceiling of the Sistine Chapel at the Vatican in Rome. The ceiling is 118 feet (36 m) long. The painting of God creating Adam (see page 251) is

one of the most famous parts of the ceiling. Michelangelo painted the picture of Adam in three days. It is 13 feet (4 m) high. The whole project took four years.

The Renaissance spread, and much of Europe came alive with a rebirth of art and culture. Many Renaissance paintings, particularly in the Netherlands, were concerned with everyday events in the lives of people. Frans Hals (1580–1666), Rembrandt van Rijn (1606–1669), and Jan Vermeer (1632–1675) were the three greatest Dutch painters. Vermeer liked to paint pictures of women with light coming from one window. He usually chose one small subject and painted with great perfection. The *Lace Maker* (see picture) is a good example. See how the yellow dress of the woman seems to give a glow to her lit face.

In the 1700s Britain became a rich country. With wealth came the encouragement of art. Portrait paint-

▼ *Christ Enthroned* **by an unknown artist about A.D. 600.**

ing became popular. Such artists as Sir Joshua Reynolds (1723–1792) and Thomas Gainsborough (1727–1788) were very much in demand for portraits of important people. John Constable (1776–1837) and J. M. W. Turner (1775–1851) were fine painters of landscapes. In Germany, Caspar David Friedrich (1774–1840) made landscape painting a form of religious art.

The center of European art moved to France in the late 1800s. The modern period of art began when the *Impressionists,* a group of young artists in Paris, began painting. They wanted to work in the open air, away from the usual studio kind of art. They had an urge to paint the pure colors of nature as they look in actual reflected light. This was done by the painter Claude Monet (1840–1926), a leader of the Impressionists of France. Most Impressionists were French.

The Impressionists began a new freedom in art. Since then, many artists have experimented with new ways of

▲ *The Lace Maker* by Jan Vermeer, the Dutch artist.

▲ *Two Men Contemplating the Moon* by Caspar David Friedrich, the German painter. Painted in 1819, it is a fine example of German Romantic art.

▼ *The Creation of Adam* by Michelangelo, painted on the ceiling of the Sistine Chapel in Rome, Italy. The artist took four years to complete the task.

▲ John Hoyland's *Acrylic on Canvas* is an example of contemporary abstract art. The viewer can make up his or her own mind about the subject.

painting. The Cubists, led by Pablo Picasso (1881–1973), were interested in abstract forms. But Picasso, unlike most painters, did not develop only one style of painting. He often changed his style completely.

Many new art styles developed in the United States after World War II. New York City is thought by many to be the world center of art, as Paris was for hundreds of years. Among U.S. painters are Winslow Homer (1836–1910), Georgia O'Keeffe (1887–1986), Jackson Pollock (1912–1956), Roy Lichtenstein (born 1923), Andy Warhol (1926–1987) and Mark Rothko (1903–1970).

▶▶▶▶ **FIND OUT MORE** ◀◀◀◀
Kinds of Art see Abstract Art; Architecture; Carving; Clay Modeling; Design; Drawing; Etching and Engraving; Folk Art; Graphic Arts; Mosaic; Painting; Paper Sculpture; Sculpture; Symbolism
Arts of Many Peoples see Dutch and Flemish Art; Greek Art; Native American Art; Maya; Oriental Art; Roman Art
Art Collections see Florence; Louvre; Vatican City; Venice
Periods of Art see Baroque Period; Impressionism; Modern Art; Renaissance; Rococo Art; Romanesque Art; Romantic Period
For individual artists see names in the Index volume

ARTHRITIS

Imagine having a pain as bad as a toothache every time you tried to bend your fingers. Picking up a spoon would be extremely difficult. That is how it feels to have arthritis, a painful disease of the joints between bones.

In healthy joints the ends of the bones are covered in *cartilage,* a rubbery substance that cushions the shocks caused by walking and other movements. The cartilage is also slip-

pery, helping the bones to slide easily across the joint.

Arthritis affects the joint and its cartilage. An *arthritic* joint has lost the use of the cartilage, either by it becoming damaged, or by it wearing away. The bones rub together painfully with every movement and there is often some swelling.

This type of arthritis is called *osteoarthritis.* The most commonly affected areas are the fingers, knees, neck, and back. Older people often get osteoarthritis, but younger people can also suffer from it if they have injured a joint.

Rheumatoid arthritis is more extreme than osteoarthritis. It also affects mainly younger people, between the ages of 20 and 40, and is three times as common in women as in men. Joints are eaten away, either by *microorganisms* or by the body's *autoimmune system,* which normally attacks infections. The joints that are affected, usually the knuckles and wrists, often become deformed.

There are more than 100 types of arthritis. One person out of every eight suffers from some form of arthritis. Unfortunately, there is no cure for any of these, but there are treatments to relieve pain and contain the spread of the disease.

Aspirin and stronger *analgesics* and steroids can lessen the pain and swelling associated with arthritis. Programs of exercise can strengthen certain joints. Surgeons can replace joints that have been destroyed by the disease.

▶▶▶▶ **FIND OUT MORE** ◀◀◀◀
Bone; Skeleton

ARTHROPOD

SEE CENTIPEDES AND MILLIPEDES, CRUSTACEAN, INSECT, SPIDER

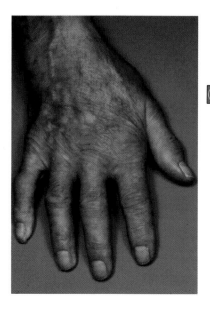

▼ Rheumatoid arthritis in a woman's hand. Joints become hot, painful, red, and swollen. Eventually the sufferer may be crippled as the hands stiffen into a deformed position.

ARTHUR, CHESTER A. (1829–1886)

After President James A. Garfield was shot on July 2, 1881, there was much talk about what would happen if Vice President Chester A. Arthur became the new President of the United States. Dishonesty in government was widespread at that time. People thought Arthur would give jobs to his friends and open the White House to loafers. But he became somewhat of a reformer.

He was born in Vermont, son of a Baptist minister. After Arthur graduated from Union College, he became a teacher, taught in a school in Vermont and later became a school principal in New York. He studied law and became a successful lawyer in New York City. Before the Civil War, he became famous for defending the civil liberties of runaway slaves.

In 1860, Arthur helped Edwin D. Morgan win reelection as the Republican governor of New York and was rewarded with the job of engineer-in-chief of the state. He reorganized the New York militia. Later President Ulysses S. Grant appointed him collector of the port of New York, a well-paid, powerful political position.

He was part of Roscoe Conkling's New York Republican machine. Though Arthur was removed by President Rutherford B. Hayes, he was given the Republican vice presidential nomination through Conkling's help. He was elected with Garfield in 1880.

After Garfield died on September 19, 1881, Arthur became the 21st President of the United States. Many Americans thought Arthur was a man who would do whatever the Republican Party wanted. The Republican Party bosses thought so, too. But they were proved wrong. Arthur tried hard to do what he thought was right for the whole country, not just for the Republicans. He changed the *spoils system*, the practice of giving the best government jobs to the most faithful supporters of the party. He also set up a merit system that gave the best jobs to those who passed difficult examinations.

Arthur made other changes, too. He reorganized and modernized the U.S. Navy. He removed dishonest men who controlled the Post Office. He worked to admit Chinese immigrants to the U.S. He called an international conference for the purpose of establishing standard time zones around the globe.

The Republican Party leaders were angry with Arthur, because he did not follow their orders. They did not nominate him for President again in 1884. But, when he retired to his New York home after four years as President, Arthur had won the respect of the nation.

▶▶▶▶ **FIND OUT MORE** ◀◀◀◀
Assassination; Garfield, James A.; Government; Careers; Presidency

**CHESTER A. ARTHUR
TWENTY-FIRST
PRESIDENT**

**SEPTEMBER 20, 1881–
MARCH 4, 1885**

Born: October 5, 1830, Fairfield, Vermont

Parents: Reverend William and Malvina Stone Arthur

Education: Union College

Religion: Episcopalian

Occupation: Teacher and Lawyer

Political Party: Republican

Married: 1859 to Ellen Lewis Herndon (1837–1880)

Children: 2 sons (1 died in infancy), 1 daughter

Died: November 18, 1886, New York City

Buried: Albany, New York

◀ **The Brooklyn Bridge was opened in 1883, during President Chester Arthur's term of office. It was hailed as the eighth wonder of the world.**

In the 15th century an Englishman called Sir Thomas Malory gathered together many of the stories about King Arthur. They appeared in a book called *Morte d'Arthur* (Death of Arthur). This book was one of the very first books printed in English by William Caxton in 1485.

▼ A Victorian painting by William Scott of the death of King Arthur. In a 12th century chronicle, Arthur is said to have died at the Battle of Camlan in 537.

ARTHUR, KING

Many old legends tell of Arthur, a strong war leader of the Celts, the people who lived in Britain 1,500 years ago, before the Saxons invaded the land in the 500s. The legends say that the country had no king for a short time in the 500s. The people prayed for help in choosing one. Suddenly a stone appeared outside a church. In the stone was stuck a sword. Men from all over the land tried to pull the sword out, but all failed. One day Arthur, the young son of the dead king, came forward and removed the sword. He was named king.

King Arthur was given another sword, called *Excalibur*, by the Lady-of-the-Lake. He ruled with his beautiful queen, Guinevere. Their castle was Tintagel, according to some legends, or Camelot, according to others. Towns all over England, Scotland, and Wales still claim to have been the site of Arthur's castle. Arthur's faithful friend and adviser was called Merlin, a poet, prophet, and magician. Arthur's knights helped bring peace to the whole country. They met with him around the famous Round Table, where all were considered equal.

Stories also tell of the wonderful deeds that King Arthur's knights carried out. But one of them, Sir Modred, was a traitor. He tried to become king. Arthur killed Modred in battle, but Arthur himself was wounded. King Arthur was carried off on a magic barge to the mysterious Isle of Avalon to be healed. According to the legend, one day Arthur will return to be king again.

Nothing is known about the real Arthur—if he existed. But the tales about Arthur, Merlin, and the Knights of the Round Table have become part of European culture and have fascinated people all over the world for centuries. Many of the world's best poets and musicians have written about this legendary hero.

▶▶▶▶ **FIND OUT MORE** ◀◀◀◀
English History; Knighthood; Legend

ARTICLE

SEE PARTS OF SPEECH

ARTICLES OF CONFEDERATION

The 13 American colonies needed some system of rules to govern themselves after the Declaration of Independence was adopted on July 4, 1776. The agreement that set up the first United States Government was called the *Articles of Confederation.*

Under the Articles, each state kept its rights but granted some powers to the Continental Congress, called the "Congress of the Confederation." Congress had power over foreign affairs, disputes among states, national defense, money, Indian affairs, and states' claims to western territory.

All states had *ratified* (accepted) the Articles of Confederation by 1781. But people soon discovered that the Articles did not give the U.S. Government enough power to run the country. Congress could only ask the states for money but could not tax them. Congress had no control over trade among states or with foreign countries. The country had no president, king, or even federal judges.

It became clear that the Articles were not working very well. It was difficult to obtain the nine votes needed from the 13 states to pass any important measure. For a few years Congress struggled on, but eventually 55 delegates assembled at Philadelphia to revise the Articles. The Constitutional Convention met in May 1787. The delegates wrote a whole new document instead—the *Constitution of the United States*. The Constitution went into effect on March 4, 1789, and is still the basic law of the United States.

▶▶▶▶ **FIND OUT MORE** ◀◀◀◀
Revolutionary War; Constitution, United States; Continental Congress; Declaration of Independence

⚙ ARTIFICIAL INTELLIGENCE

People often say that computers can be *programmed* to do nearly everything that human beings can do. But computer specialists know that one thing that computers cannot do is think for themselves. The specialists are constantly trying to develop this ability, which is known as *artificial intelligence* or A.I.

Even the most advanced computers can only follow a sequence of steps written down in the computer program. A computer with artificial intelligence would start with that information, but would be able to add more by itself.

The research into this exciting area of computer science is rewarding, but takes time. Imagine trying to write a computer program that would tell a computer how to see. That is just the sort of work being done with *computer vision systems*. Experiments in this area are linking computers with cameras. The aim is to teach computers to see and recognize shapes.

Similar research into artificial intel-

ligence has led to some advances in how computers could be taught to "hear." People with injuries or poor typing skills could then use the computer by speaking and would not need the keyboard. A computer with the ability to see, hear, and think could even act as a guardian. It could call the police if it saw a crime or if an elderly person was injured at home.

Some of the biggest breakthroughs in A.I. have been related to industry. One of these is in the area of *expert systems*. The computer is programmed to follow the way an expert would think about a particular subject.

Using an expert system, a computer might be given information about the number of people who bought a particular brand of ice cream in August. The computer then tells how to improve the ice cream's quality, of which people are likely to buy more, and how to advertise the improved product. Having the computer *software* for such a system would be like hiring an expert in the field.

Computer-Aided Design (CAD) and *Computer-Aided Manufacture* (CAM) are two other important areas of A.I. These enable companies to find the most efficient way to organize their equipment. The two processes can be linked to create a CAD/CAM system.

These systems can also make life more interesting for factory workers. Factory workers often do the same job every day on an *assembly line*. This type of routine is very boring and can lead to illness or industrial accidents. A CAD/CAM solution might show how people can take certain jobs in turn, or together in groups.

Many advances have already been made in artificial intelligence by computer specialists. However, people still look forward to the time when computers will really have the ability to think for themselves.

▲ **"Ghengis" is a robot made to perform very simple tasks. Ghengis can follow basic logic rules to chase any moving objects nearby. Research like this may lead to future industrial robots checking and repairing machines inaccessible to humans.**

▶▶▶▶ **FIND OUT MORE** ◀◀◀◀
Computer; Microprocessor

▲ A special type of respiratory first aid is used when a person has had a heart attack. It is called cardiopulmonary resuscitation (CPR) and must be done by trained people. The victim is given mouth-to-mouth resuscitation, and at the same time, the reviver must perform a massage on the victim's chest to encourage blood to keep flowing through the body.

ARTIFICIAL RESPIRATION

Anyone who stops breathing will usually die in four to six minutes. Drowning, electric shock, gas poisoning, misuse of drugs, or other causes can stop a person's breathing. Artificial respiration, done the right way, may save a life.

Mouth-to-mouth breathing is one way to try and help a person start breathing again. This treatment gets more air into the lungs than do other methods. The first step is to turn the victim's head to the side. Clean out the mouth. Take out anything that can keep air from going in. Put one hand on the forehead and the other hand under the neck. Tip the head way back, so that the injured person's tongue won't block the air passage.

Pinch the nose shut. Take a deep breath, open your mouth wide, and put it over the victim's mouth. Make a tight seal. Blow to fill up the lungs. Blow hard, as if you are blowing air into a balloon. Watch the chest rise. Then turn your head aside and listen for air to come out. Watch the chest fall. Do these two steps over and over, once every five seconds. Keep doing this, at your normal breathing pace, listening until the victim begins breathing normally.

If you have to help a baby to start breathing again, tip the head back gently—not so far as for an adult. A baby's face is small, so you may not be able to make a seal over the mouth alone or nose alone. Put your mouth over the baby's mouth and nose. Blow gently, with small puffs of air. Blow more often—once every three seconds. Say, "Blow-listen-breathe," to a count of three.

Don't give up if the victim doesn't start breathing right away. You may have to try for a long time. Keep on trying until a help arrives.

An improved method of artificial respiration called *cardiopulmonary resuscitation* (CPR) can be learned from Red Cross personnel.

▶ ▶ ▶ ▶ **FIND OUT MORE** ◀ ◀ ◀ ◀
First Aid; Lifesaving

QUIZ ANSWERS

American History quiz, page 143
1. George III.
2. First New York City (1789 to 1790); Philadelphia (1790 to 1800).
3. Los Angeles means "the angels."
4. An escape route for runaway slaves.
5. Hawaii (1959).

Ancient Civilizations quiz, page 160
1. The Phoenicians. The Greeks improved it.
2. Crete, an island near Greece.
3. The Hippocratic oath, after Hippocrates, who founded a school of medicine and a code of ethics (rules) that doctors still follow today.
4. Bronze.

Animal Kingdom quiz, page 176
1. Alligators.
2. The domestic cat, lion, tiger, leopard, jaguar, cougar, wildcat, lynx, cheetah.
3. The male stays with the eggs for 64 days.
4. *Omnivorous.* The name means "all-eating."

Arithmetic quiz, page 231
1. First, second, third, etc.
2. Multiply .05 x 30, which equals 1.50, or $1.50. Add this to the $5.00 you first put in the bank. After 30 days you have $6.50.
3. Divide 30 by 3 (10). Subtract 10 from 30 to find that Susie got there in 20 minutes.
4. 30 x 1½ can be written as 30 x 1.5. Multiply this. It took her 45 minutes.